THE FIRST GERMANS IN AMERICA

With a Biographical
Directory of
New York Germans

Edited By

Don Heinrich Tolzmann

HERITAGE BOOKS, INC.

Other Books By The Author:

Germany and America, 1450-1700

Published 1992 By

HERITAGE BOOKS, INC.
1540E Pointer Ridge Place, Bowie, Maryland 20716
(301)-390-7709

ISBN 1-55613-547-5

CONTENTS

iii

PREFACE

The purpose of this work is to provide information on the first Germans in America, as well as to identify and establish the actual beginning date of German-American history. The editor would like to express gratitude to Dr. Robert E. Ward, Baldwin-Wallace College, for reviewing the final draft of the manuscript, as well as for the additional bibliographical references he provided.

Don Heinrich Tolzmann
University of Cincinnati

INTRODUCTION

In 1983, the tricentennial of the establishment of the first permanent German settlement in America at Germantown, Pennsylvania, was celebrated with considerable fanfare, pomp, and circumstance.[1]

Since that time there has been a veritable avalanche of publications dealing with many aspects of German-American history, literature, and culture at the national, regional, and local levels.[2] Contributing greatly to this were the ethnic revival and increased interest in roots and heritage, as well as the 1980 US Census, which reported that the German element was the nation's largest ethnic group.[3] This national interest in the German heritage found expression in 1987 with a presidential proclamation of the first national German-American Day.[4] The date for this celebration is, of course, the sixth of October, the date in 1683 on which Germantown, Pennsylvania, was founded.

1683 is therefore a key date in German-American annals, but is it the beginning date of German-American history? The answer is definitely not. It was in 1608 that Germans first arrived in America, at Jamestown, Virginia. Within a few years, Germans began joining the Dutch settlement of New Netherland (later New York) and other communities in the colonies. Unlike the Germantown settlers, the pre-1683 German immigrants did not come as a group of families under the leadership of an organization.

As this editor has pointed out in *Germany and America (1450-1700)*, many historians begin their histories with the establishment of the first German settlements rather than adequately treating the earliest German arrivals. Indeed, many of them completely overlook the pre-1683 immigrants. It is with these immigrants that such histories should begin.[5]

The prominent German-American historian, Wilhelm Kaufmann, recognized this serious limitation in German-American histories.[6]

The purpose of the present volume is twofold: first, to draw attention to and fix the date of the actual beginning of German-American history; second, to provide information on the grossly neglected pre-1683 period. To accomplish these aims, this editor has selected three important works originally published in the early 1900s which have escaped consideration by many scholars.[7]

Chapter 1, by Otto Lohr, provides an overview of the first Germans in the colonies, while Chapter 2, by Herrmann Schuricht, focuses on the first Germans in Virginia. Chapter 3, by John O. Evjen, concentrates on the first Germans in New Netherland/New York. In this volume, these works are presented as a facsimile reprint of the originals.

The particular value of these works is that they not only shed light on the first Germans in America, but also provide names with biographical information. The present volume contains an index to the several hundred names of the pre-1683 group listed in these three works.

It is perhaps more than mere coincidence that four important histories of the Germans in America were in the process of publication in 1908, the 300th anniversary of the arrival of the first Germans in America. Indeed, the title of one of them *Drei Jahrhunderte deutschen Lebens in*

Amerika (Three Centuries of German Life in America), by Rudolf Cronau, points toward such a commemoration.[8] This publication appeared in 1909, the same year that Albert B. Faust's standard history was published.[9] The other two, by Georg von Bosse and Max Heinrici,[10] demonstrate that the 300th anniversary of the arrival of the first Germans in America (1608-1908) was a major event in the pre-World War I German-American community.[11]

The war caused this event and many other aspects of German-Americana to be obscured and even forgotten. In the 1980s only the commemoration of the Germantown settlement drew the attention of German-American organizations and writers. The 300th anniversary of the founding of the first German settlement was widely celebrated in 1983. Five years later, the first protest in America against slavery (issued at Germantown in 1688) was the subject of a tricentennial celebration.[12] Thus, one can point to three tricentennial celebrations in the twentieth century (1908, 1983, and 1988).

This editor has long believed that the arrival of the first Germans in 1608 should also be the subject of national attention and celebration. It is time to begin extensive planning for the 400th anniversary of the arrival of the first Germans in America. It will be a long time until the quadricentennial of the Germantown settlement in 2083, an event a future generation should commemorate. But the Jamestown Germans' celebration is only seventeen years off. Why not associate the two events by holding the 400th anniversary of the first Germans in America on October 6, 2008?

It is hoped that this work will be useful as a basic reference source to aid in such preparation and that it will encourage the inclusion of the earliest period of German-American history in future publications and school curricula.

NOTES

1. With regard to the 1983 German-American Tricentennial, see Don Heinrich Tolzmann, "Celebrating the German Heritage," *Yearbook of German-American Studies*, 18(1983): 1-5.
2. For a bibliography of works published since the 1983 Tricentennial, see Margit B. Krewson, *Immigrants from the German-Speaking Countries of Europe: A Selective Bibliography* (Washington, D.C.: Library of Congress, 1991). Krewson lists here 247 works.
3. For information about the 1980 Census, see Don Heinrich Tolzmann, "The 1980 Census and the German Element," *Society for German-American Studies Newsletter*, 5:2(1984): 2.
4. The history of the annual German-American Day Celebration, which began in 1987, can be found in the editor's *In der Neuen Welt: Deutsch-Amerikanische Festschrift fuer die 500-Jahrfeier der Entdeckung von Amerika* (New York: Peter Lang Pub. Co., 1992).
5. See Don Heinrich Tolzmann, *Germany and America (1450-1700): Julius Friedrich Sachse's History of the German Role in the Discovery, Exploration and Settlement of the New World* (Bowie, Maryland: Heritage Books, Inc., 1991).
6. Wilhelm Kaufmann, *Die Deutschen im amerikanischen Buergerkriege (Sezessionskrieg 1861-1865)* (Muenchen: R. Oldenbourg, 1911), pp. 579-81.

7. Lohr's chapter originally appeared in: Otto Lohr, *The First Germans in North America and the German Element of New Netherland* (New York: G.E. Stechert, 1912); Schuricht's appeared in: Herrmann Schuricht, *History of the German Element of Virginia* (Baltimore: Kroh, 1898); and Evjen's appeared in: John O. Evjen, *Scandinavian Immigrants in New York, 1630-1674* (Minneapolis: Holter, 1916).

8. See Rudolph Cronau, *Drei Jahrhunderte deutschen Lebens in Amerika. Eine Geschichte der Deutschen in den Vereinigten Staaten* (Berlin: Dietrich Reimer, 1909).

9. See Albert F. Faust, *The German Element in the United States* (Boston: Houghton Mifflin Co., 1909).

10. See Georg von Bosse, *Das deutsche Element in den Vereinigten Staaten* (Stuttgart: Chr. Beisersche Verlagsbuchhandlung, 1908) and Max Heinrici, *Das Buch der Deutschen in Amerika* (Philadelphia: German-American National Alliance, 1909).

11. For an annotated bibliography of the works cited in footnotes 8-10 see Don Heinrich Tolzmann, *Catalog of the German-Americana Collection, University of Cincinnati* (Munich: K.G. Saur, 1990), vol. 1, pp. 53-72.

12. Regarding the 1988 tricentennial, see "Transcription of Germantown Friends' Protest Against Slavery, 1688," *Yearbook of German-American Studies*, 23(1988): 219-22. Also see the definitive work dealing with Pastorius, Marion Dexter Learned, *The Life of Francis Daniel Pastorius: The Founder of Germantown* (Philadelphia: William J. Campbell, 1908). Also note that Learned brought his history out in 1908 in commemoration of the arrival of the first German settlers in America in 1608.

OTHER WORKS BY THE EDITOR

German-Americana: A Bibliography. Scarecrow Press, 1975.

America's German Heritage. German-American National Congress, 1976.

German-American Literature. Scarecrow Press, 1977.

Festschrift for the German-American Tricentennial Jubilee: Cincinnati 1983. Cincinnati Historical Society, 1982.

The Cincinnati Germans after the Great War. Peter Lang Publishing Co., 1987.

The First Description of Cincinnati and Other Ohio Settlements: The Travel Report of Johann Heckewelder, 1792. University Press of America, 1988.

Spring Grove and Its Creator: H.A. Rattermann's Biography of Adolph Strauch. Ohio Book Store, 1988.

Catalog of the German-Americana Collection, University of Cincinnati. K. G. Saur, 1990.

The First Mayor of Cincinnati: George A. Katzenberger's Biography of Major David Ziegler. University Press of America, 1990.

New German-American Studies. Peter Lang Publishing Co., 1990- .

Germany and America (1450-1700): Julius Friedrich Sachse's History of the German Role in the Discovery, Exploration and Settlement of the New World. Heritage Books, Inc., 1991.

In der Neuen Welt: Deutsch-Amerikanische Festschrift fuer die 500-Jahrfeier der Entdeckung von Amerika. Peter Lang Publishing Co., 1992.

1. THE FIRST GERMANS IN AMERICA

By

Otto Lohr

This chapter is a facsimile of material which originally appeared in Otto Lohr's *The First Germans in North America and the German Element of New Netherland*, New York: G.E. Stechert, 1912.

ROM the beginning of the seventeenth century Germans are found scattered all along the Atlantic coast of North America. Though fate had allotted but a secondary role to these contemporaries of the Thirty Years' War under these skies, it could not prevent the participation of a considerable number of them in the opening of the northern half of the New World and the transplanting of European civilization into the American colonies. These earliest representatives of American Germandom, most of whom, after a life full of toil and struggle, had found eternal rest, at the time when the first purely German settlement was made in Germantown, Pennsylvania, constitute a stratum of typical American pioneer life. Considering their achievements on the whole, as well as such as are individually noteworthy, and also the characteristic German traits in their life work, these pioneers compare favorably with their fellow settlers of early colonial times and therefore demand adequate recognition in history. Whether present in limited numbers, or living in moderate circumstances, chroniclers do not fail to narrate special incidents of these early Germans. The real German work of this epoch covers little more than a generation. Of those who accomplished it, some were leaders in colonization and officers, a few explorers of the country and settlement pioneers. Some of them were the first in various callings of new-land management. The majority of the Germans, to whom had been assigned tasks of everyday life, were well qualified to perform the fundamental labor of civilization and pioneer economics. Besides solving work-a-day problems, the creation of an institution which actually represents the beginning of German life on American soil is to be considered as not the least of their merits.

Introductory Note.—This paper is the first attempt to sketch the beginnings of German immigration in the North American colonies connectedly and on a broad basis. New Netherland being the first conspicuous goal of German influx, naturally had to be treated as extensively as the limited space of a preliminary outline would permit. The remainder claims neither originality in each and every detail, nor completeness. And yet, more than half of what is presented in the following pages will undoubtedly be new to readers familiar with the story of German life and strife in this country.

VIRGINIA

Jamestown, Virginia, the cradle of Anglo-Saxon America, is the place, where Germans are met with for the first time. The earliest incidents on record are cases of imported contract laborers Those sent to Virginia in 1608 were skilled workmen, glass-blowers. Captain John Smith, characterizing his men, gives the following account of them: " . . labourers . . that neuer did know what a dayes worke was: except the Dutch-men and Poles, and some dozen other . . "[1] In 1620 four mill-wrights from Hamburg were sent to the same settlement, to erect saw-mills;[2] in England timber was still sawed by hand.[3] The Germans who settled in the Cavalier colony in larger numbers about the middle of the seventeenth century, seem to have been attracted chiefly by the profitable tobacco business. The most highly educated citizen of Northampton County in 1657 was, perhaps, Dr. Georg Nicolaus Hacke, a native of Cologne.[4] Thomas Harmanson, founder of one of the most prominent Eastern Shore families, a native of Brandenburg, was naturalized October 24, 1684, by an act of assembly.[5] Johann Sigismund Cluverius, owner of a considerable estate in York County, was ostensibly also of German birth.[6]

---

[1] John Smith, The Generall Historie of Virginia, New-England, the Summer Isles, London, 1624, p. 94.

[2] The Records of the Virginia Company, ed. S. M. Kingsbury, Washington, 1906, I, pp. 368, 372, 428.

[3] Edward Eggleston, The Beginners of a Nation, New York, 1896, p. 82.

[4] Philip Alexander Bruce, Social Life of Virginia in the Seventeenth Century, Richmond, Va., 1907, p. 260.

[5] William and Mary College Quarterly, ed. L. G. Tyler. Williams-burg, Va., I, 1892, p. 192. Bruce, Social Life of Va., p. 261, incorrectly gives 1622 as the year of Harmanson's naturalization.

[6] Bruce, p. 260.

NEW ENGLAND

The first Germans of New England arrived, as far as we know, with the founders of Massachusetts Bay Colony in 1630. The proof of this fact, as well as of the influence of this first small group, is found in one of the most important pamphlets published in connection with New England colonization, "The Planter's Plea" (1630). This tract, published in London shortly after the departure of Winthrop's Puritan fleet, and supposed to have been written by John White, the "patriarch of Dorchester" and the "father of Massachusetts Bay Colony," contains the following statement: "It is not improbable that, partly for their sakes, and partly for respect to some Germans that are gone over with them, and more that intend to follow after, even those which otherwise would not much desire innovation of themselves, yet for the maintaining of peace and unity (the only solder of a weak, unsettled body) will be won to consent to some variation from the forms and customs of our church . . ." Some of the early New England Germans got there via New Amsterdam; we find them in Connecticut, Rhode Island, Boston, etc. In 1661 the ship-surgeon Spoeri from Zurich in Switzerland paid a visit to Rhode Island. His narrative of New England is one of the few of German pen on early American colonial times still extant.[7] The influence of Germans from afar it was that stimulated the intellectual life of New England, at a certain period in its heroic days: the active German circle about Milton (and the friends of Comenius), to which are accredited the first steps in the founding of the Royal Society, Haak, Hartlib, and Oldenburg. Among the letters exchanged between London (the Continent respectively) and New England, there is one by Oldenburg, written in 1669, from which a significant passage deserves to be quoted. Thus writes the first secretary of the Royal Society to the younger Winthrop, Governor of Connecticut: "It would contribute much to ye increase of ye honor of yt people to keep in their Archives ye faithfull records of all their successes, stops, exigencies, from their beginnings, and to doe the like kindness for their neighbors, as New Netherland or the Main or Georgeana; for ye L^d

---

[7] Americanische Reissbeschreibung Nach den Caribes Insslen Und Neu-Engelland. Verrichtet und aufgesetzt durch Felix-Christian Spoeri, Zurich, 1677.

[5]

Ploydens Plantaon, Maryland, Virgin.; and ye many Islands about yt continent, as hath been noted."[8]

NEW SWEDEN

In New Sweden, for the foundation and development of which Gustavus Adolphus and after his death Oxenstierna had taken initial steps on German soil, and the European management of which rested in the hands of a German treasurer and a German bookkeeper, there were a few Germans among its officials during the seventeen years of its existence (1638-1655). There were also a number of German colonists, chiefly soldiers; however, according to recent researches these were not as numerous, as had formerly been supposed. The first governor was Peter Minuit from Wesel; his brother-in-law, Hendrick Huygen from Cleves, was commissary during and after Minuit's term of office. From 1640-1643 a young officer, Peter Hollender Ridder, very likely a German, was at the head of the colony. The last factor of New Sweden was Henrich von Elswich, a merchant from Lubeck. In the lists of the inhabitants of the settlements, Amandus Johnson, the most recent historian of New Sweden[9], has found but few Germans expressly mentioned as such. The greater part of these belonged to the garrisons of the forts, among them a few from Hamburg, one from Holstein, one from Stralsund, one from Brandenburg, one from Koenigsberg and one from Reval. As is obvious, the majority of these men came from cities and provinces where Usselinx had visited and worked in the interest of his transatlantic colonization scheme.[10] There still remain such as have names unmistakably pointing to German origin; not many; two or three dozen at the most. Accordingly the probable ratio between Germans and Swedes,etc., in New Sweden would be 1:10. (This has reference only to the Germans coming over with the Swedes; along with the colonization of New Netherland, undoubtedly a number of Germans

[8]Massachusetts Historical Society, Proceedings, Vol. XVI, 1878, Boston, 1879, p. 241.

[9]Amandus Johnson, The Swedish Settlements on the Delaware, New York, 1911, 2 vols.

[10]J. Franklin Jameson, Willem Usselinx. American Historical Association, Papers, Vol. II, 1887.

also struck New Swedish territory). Unfortunately Johnson has nothing or very little to say about the distribution of the various nationalities. The following remark is of some importance: "The instructions of the officers were written in Swedish, German and Dutch. The Dutch and German officers, soldiers and settlers were able to converse in Swedish, and they gradually became fairly well versed in the language, but all the account books and most of the bills preserved to us are written in Dutch or German."[11] The Labadists, Dankers and Sluyter, the latter a German from Wesel (recte Vorstmann), in search of a place of refuge for their sect, longing to leave Europe, traversed the colonies from Massachusetts to Maryland, eagerly taking notes, and came to the Delaware in 1679. There they met several Germans, mostly Holsteiners, especially Otto Ernst Koch, "late medicus", one of the justices on the Delaware and proprietor of Tinicum Island.[12] When Pastorius came to Pennsylvania he found "a few High Germans . . who had already inhabited this country for twenty years, and had become naturalized so to say; these were Silesians, Brandenburgers, Holsteiners, Swiss, etc. Also one from Nuremberg, named Jan Jaquet."[13] The latter, Jean Paul Jacquet, for years agent of the West India Company in Brazil, after the departure of the Swedes, had been made vice-director on the South River (as the Dutch called the Delaware in contradistinction to the North River, the Hudson). In 1674 he was appointed a justice of the court at New Castle.[14]

---

[11] Johnson, p. 548.

[12] Journal of a Voyage to New York and a Tour in Several of the American Colonies in 1679-80. By Jasper Dankers and Peter Sluyter. Translated by Henry C. Murphy, Brooklyn, 1867, p. 174-187.

[13] F. D. Pastorius, Sichere Nachricht auss America, 1684. Photographic Reproduction in M. D. Learned's The Life of Francis Daniel Pastorius, Philadelphia, 1908, p. 128.

[14] Narratives of Early Pennsylvania, West New Jersey and Delaware, 1630-1707. Ed. Albert Cook Myers. New York, 1912, p. 400.

MARYLAND

Most of the early German settlers of Maryland came from Virginia, New Netherland and New Sweden. The best known are the Herrman and Hacke families, and Johann Lederer. Augustin Herrman, who spent the most important time of his life in New Amsterdam, is known as the first surveyor of Maryland and designer of the first map of Lord Baltimore's colony; for this work he was granted a large tract of land in Cecil County (Bohemia Manor).[15] Johann Lederer, a native of Hamburg, who immortalized himself as the discoverer of the Virginia Valley, was naturalized in 1671. The Labadists during their travels in Maryland met a settler named Commegys from Vienna and at a plantation "a person who spoke high Dutch . . a kind of proctor or advocate in the courts."

CAROLINA

The first German of renown who set foot on Carolina soil was Johann Lederer. This was in 1670. In the following year, perhaps in connection with his exploring tours, the colony "received a great addition to its strength" from Dutch people of New York. According to Bernheim,[16] who claims he has his information from the old chroniclers, the majority of these Dutch were Lutherans. This, if true, would partly explain the disappearance of a number of German Lutherans from New York about this period.

---

[15] The best monograph on Herrman is H. A. Rattermann's in Deutsch-Amerikanisches Magazin, I, 1886, p. 202 ff.

[16] G. D. Bernheim, History of the German Settlements and of the Lutheran Church in North and South Carolina. Philadelphia, 1872, p. 64-65.

NEW NETHERLAND

Of all early North American colonies, New York only and solely possessed a German population numerically noteworthy and almost within reach of exact research. This province and the city by the same name, prior to 1664 New Netherland and New Amsterdam—it must be remembered, however, the former at a time comprised greater or smaller portions of what were later Connecticut and New Jersey—was the chief goal of German immigration during the middle third of the seventeenth century.

The first white settler within the limits of the present State of New York was Henrich Christiansen from the German city of Cleves.[17] And he, the very first of all German-American pioneers, it was who continued and completed the work begun by Henry Hudson; while the latter is looked upon as the discoverer, the former must be considered the explorer of the Hudson River territory.[18] His eleven trips to the mouth of the Hudson, following almost immediately Hudson's voyage of discovery, represent our present transatlantic traffic in its incipiency. He built the first dwellings and prepared the road to the chief source of income of the colony, the fur trade. His tragic death deprived him not only of the fruits of his labor, but also of a good deal of his renown after death: no place bears his name.[19]

The beginnings of civil order and organized work of civilization on Manhattan Island are connected with the name of Peter Minuit. This first general-director of New Netherland, apparently of French descent, had come from Wesel; however his personality and his official life show the imprints of Dutch culture[20] (in New Netherland as well as at a later period in New Sweden). Under Minuit's leadership the trading-post, the rendezvous of traders and hunters, which heretofore had been obliged to get its supply of provisions from "Patria," became a plantation in a twofold sense of the word, a self-supporting agricultural colony. Among his officials and soldiers, among the traders and farmers we find Germans.

---

[17] Joannes de Laet, Nieuwe Wereldt, Leyden, 1625, p. 88.
[18] Niclaes a Wassenaer, Historisch Verhael, Amsterdam, 1624, p. 85.
[19] "No Mans Land" formerly was called Hendrick Christiaensen's Eyland.
[20] Minuit writes "good Dutch though with distinctly German spelling."
A. J. F. van Laer, Van Rensselaer Bowier Manuscripts. Albany, 1908, p. 31.

During Minuit's administration Rensselaerswyck was founded near Fort Orange (Albany), under the patroonship of Kiliaen van Rensselaer and his partners. The human material which formed the foundation of the present State capital, may not have been the worst that came to the new world, since it was selected by the cautious merchant of Amsterdam himself. With some degree of certainty the native places of about one and a half hundred adult male immigrants are ascertained—out of a sum total of not quite 250—reaching here between 1630 and 1653. More than one half came from the provinces of the Netherlands (the Spanish dominions included). The Germans constitute somewhat less than one fourth. The Scandinavians and English together (including one Irishman and one Scotchman) are about one seventh. One Frenchman and one Croatian complete this heterogeneous crowd.[2]

At the close of the fourth decade, when "settlers of excellent quality" (Fiske) flocked into New Netherland, the current of German immigration becomes visible in a marked degree. This influx, continuing for over a quarter of a century, furnishes the first perceptible group of German-American population. Their assimilation took place within the scope of Dutch colonizing; the Thirty Year's War lent it the dreary background. At that time the attention of the German countries had been roused in the direction of New Netherland. Usselinx' recruiting visits to the cities of the North and Baltic Sea Coasts from Emden to Reval, were not in vain, nor had he appealed to German princes and conventions unsuccessfully. New Sweden, for which money and men were wanted, lay in the same course as New Netherland. Similarly as John Maurice of Nassau, governor of Brazil, in 1637 advised the Dutch West India Company to settle German exiles, seeking refuge in Holland, in South America,[2] the Count of Solms had considered the idea of settling his subjects driven out of the County of Solms by the war, in New Netherland.[3] The

---

[2]New York State Education Department, New York State Library, Van Rensselaer Bowier Manuscripts. Translated and edited by A. J. F. van Laer, Archivist. Albany, 1908, p. 805-846.

[3]Caspar Barlaeus, Brasilianische Geschichte, Cleves, 1659, p. 136, 137.

[3]Documents relative to the Colonial History of the State of New York, ed. E. B. O'Callaghan, Albany, Vol. I, 1856, p. 118.

revocation of the fur trade monopoly in 1639, followed by a revival in New Netherland affairs, drew many a German from the Hansa cities to Manhattan.

A means to approximately estimate the German element of New Amsterdam is found in some sort of semi-official statistics. Although these statistics do not embrace the total population, a ratio can be deduced. This means is the Marriage Records of the Reformed Dutch Church, which have fortunately been preserved.[24] This list contains for the years 1639-1664, the period of Dutch rule, the names and native places of 626 immigrants. Of these, with a certain degree of definiteness, 123 are found to be of German origin (among them 12 German couples). Accordingly the Germans would amount to not quite one fifth of the number of immigrants.[25]

The center of German life, flourishing more and more, as years went on, was, since the close of the forties, the Lutheran congregation of New Amsterdam, which beginning with the fifties more or less successfully combated the Dutch Calvinistic intolerance. Leader and adviser of the German Lutherans was Paul Schrick of Nuremberg, a well-to-do merchant. It was he who "became a chief promoter of this work," ending in the calling of the first Lutheran pastor.[26] The earliest records of this Lutheran organization, the nucleus of St. Matthews Church of to-day, have disappeared. So much we learn from contemporary documents: the leading personages active in building up the congregation and in the struggles with the predominant Reformed

[24]Records of the Reformed Dutch Church in New Amsterdam and New York. Marriage Records from 11 December, 1639, to 26 August, 1801. Ed. Samuel S. Purple, M. D., New York, 1890.

[25]In the Annual Report of the American Historical Association for the Year 1909, Washington 1911, Ruth Putnam (The Dutch Element in the United States, p. 205-218) examines the same source, with regard to its ethnical composition, arriving at figures, however, which are open to criticism. Her statement shows 16 Germans in the first hundred marriage applicants, 1639-1643; in the second hundred she finds 9 (I find 11); in the third hundred 9 (instead of 16); in the fourth 10 (instead of 17); in the fifth 6-8 (instead of 12); in the sixth 5-6 (instead of 19). Hence about 58 Germans, instead of 91, according to my figures, from the close of 1639 to the middle of 1659.

[26]Ecclesiastical Records, State of New York. Published by the State under the supervision of Hugh Hastings, State Historian, Albany, Vol. I, 1901, p. 429.

Dutch Church were Germans, the pastors, Gutwasser, Fabricius and Arens were all Germans (with the exception of a Swedish supply preacher), the majority of the members of the congregation were Germans[27], the German language was looked upon as evidence of membership[28], it is not improbable that at times German was used during service.[29]

As is the case to this very day, the early Germans of New York were a medley of all classes of society. There we find the enterprising man of fortune and the adventurous fellow without means, merchants and mechanics, professional men, farmers, sailors, soldiers, servants. These people hailed from all parts of German speaking Europe, even from Switzerland, Austria and the Baltic provinces of Russia. Three quarters of them were Low-Germans, more or less related to the Dutch in tongue and custom, and therefore readily at ease and at home. In these audacious and world-wise, industrious and sober-minded men from the German sea-coast, from East Friesland, Oldenburg, Sleswick-Holstein, Hanover, Westphalia, and the Rhenish countries, there glowed the same spirit and strove the same vigor which had brought maritime pursuits and commerce of the Hanseatic League to such prominence and had raised their citizens to such an eminent state of power and culture. Important beyond their number these Germans seem when the manifold achievements and merits of their chief representatives or of certain sets are considered. The specifically German qualities proved particularly momentous in aiding the formative

---

[27] The list of the first members, as far as it can be reconstructed, shows 28 names. mostly heads of families. There is documentary proof of 12 being Germans: Paul Schrick, Martin Hoffmann, Christian Nissen, Hermann Eduardsen, Lorenz Andriesen (Van Buskirck), Lucas Eldersen, Hermann Jansen, Johann Cornelissen, David Wessels. Heinrich Heinrichs, Meinrad Barentsen, Hermann Schmeemann. Matthias Capito, first signer of the Lutheran petition of October 10, 1657, without question was German. Of the remaining petitioners as far as they were not mentioned above, Jochem Beeckman undoubedtly like all the other Beekmans in New Netherland was of German origin; Claes de Wit according to some writers came from Westphalia. Hans Dreper, Andries Rees, George Hanel do not seem to be either Hollandish or Scandinavian. For list of petitioners see: Ecclesiastical Records, State of New York, p. 406.

[28] Ecclesiastical Records, State of New York, p. 429.

[29] At least one is justified to infer this from a passage in Charles Wooley's A two years Journal in New York, London, 1701, p. 84-85.

work of the ruling Dutch-English stock. A German trait was their religious sentiment, the loyalty to Lutheran creed, which wrested the first concessions of tolerance from official Calvinism; a German trait the Hanseatic spirit of enterprise in affairs great and small, German their interest in the welfare of the community, their tendency toward progressiveness and independence, which shook the oppressive bars of bureaucratic tutelage and patriarchal privileges.

"Perhaps no class among the early residents of New Amsterdam was more distinguished for the rapid strides they made to wealth and social distinction, in their adopted home, than those who came from the old commercial cities in Germany. The most prominent representative of this class—which included among others, the heads of the Van der Beeck, Santford, Ebbing, Leisler and Schrick families,—was Nicholas De Meyer, a native of Hamburg."[30] In this list Augustin Herrman is omitted, perhaps the most remarkable among these prosperous merchants. The story of his life and deeds reveals interesting intercolonial relations, both political and economic. By marriage he was related to Schrick and Hacke.

Leader of the progressive citizens in their fight against Kieft and Stuyvesant was (with Cornelis Melyn) a German, Jochem Petersen Kuyter, from Ditmarschen. Among the officials of the provincial and municipal government we find (in addition to those already mentioned) several Germans, viz., Ulrich Lupold from Stade, Gysbert Opdyck from Wesel, Willem Beekman, descendant of a Cologne family, born in Holland. The last-named, as also Nicolaus Meyer, was under English rule mayor of the city of New York.

The ship-surgeon and colonial physician of German origin figures widely in New World records and relations of the sixteenth and seventeenth centuries. We also meet at least a dozen of them in the early days of North America; in New Netherland Hans Kierstede from Magdeburg, Paul van der Beek from Bremen, Wilhelm Trophagen from Lemgo, and others. A man

---

[30] The New York Genealogical and Biographical Record, New York. Vol. IX, 1878, p. 13. (Contributions to the History of the ancient families of New York. By Edwin R. Purple).

of judicial learning was Hieronymus Ebbing from Hamburg, son-in-law of the Dutch historian Johannes de Laet. Tillman van Vleck from Bremen was a notary public at New Amsterdam. German by birth were the schoolmasters Jacob Joosten at Esopus-Kingston and Engelbert Steinhausen, at Bergen. Hans Stein, apparently also a German, was licensed to keep school at New Amsterdam. The first teacher of the Latin school was Alexander Carl Curtius from Lithuania. One or the other of the ministers of the Reformed Church seems to have been of German birth or descent.

Of course, one does not go wrong looking for Germans in the sound middle class, among mechanics and smaller business-men. Three of the most frequently mentioned old New Yorkers of this category are the tavernkeeper "Sergeant" Litscho from Coeslin in Pomerania,[a] the blacksmith Burger Jorissen from Hirschberg in Silesia,[aa] and the cordwainer Johann Harberdink from Bocholt in Westphalia, in whose honor John Street, New York, bears its name and from whose legacy the Dutch Reformed Church draws a princely revenue.

Quite a number of families flourishing in this country to-day—as is obvious from one or the other previous instance—date back to the unassuming German immigrants of the New Netherland epoch, the German Knickerbocker stock. Good old names among them, no longer recognizable as German, as their bearers have for generations divested themselves of everything German, families which have intermarried with the best of the continent; so for instance the Beekman, Brower, van Buskirck, Bussing, Carmer, Ditmars, Dyckman, Hoffman, Kierstede, Low, Messler, Meyer, van Norstrand, Opdyke, Remsen, Schoonmaker, Schureman, Swits, Ten Broeck, Traphagel, Wessel and Zabriskie families.

---

[a] J. H. Innes, New Amsterdam and its People, New York, 1902, p. 267 ff.
[aa] Innes, p. 223 ff.

SUMMARY

The conclusions to be drawn from this treatise suggest a re-arrangement of the first century of German-American history:

1. Sporadic appearance of Germans in the North American colonies, beginning with 1608.

2. Continuity in German immigration, regular arrivals in New Netherland and distribution among the neighboring colonies, intercolonial relations, first attempt at organization, 1637-1664.

3. Beginning of sectarian immigration and founding of a distinct German settlement in Germantown, Pennsylvania, 1683.

4. The great tide of German immigration, setting in with the exodus of the "Palatines," in 1709.

2. THE FIRST GERMANS IN VIRGINIA

By

Herrmann Schuricht

This chapter is a facsimile of material which originally appeared in Herrmann Schuricht's *History of the German Element of Virginia*, Baltimore: Kroh, 1898.

The early immigration of Germans to Virginia differs essentially, it must be admitted, from that under the leadership of Wm. Penn and Franz Pastorius to Pennsylvania, for unlike these it was not organized or compact. With the forenamed there came at once a large number of Germans to the New World, numerous additions followed and they kept together and founded German settlements which have preserved their national character to this day. But into Virginia the Germans immigrated singly, without a leader of their own nationality and without connection among themselves. Not until the beginning of the eighteenth century a German mass-immigration commenced from North Carolina, Pennsylvania, New Jersey and the Fatherland. The first comers scattered during the first decades of the colony over all its various sections, and yet the influence of this immigration proved of the greatest value to the development of Virginia or "Attanough Komouch," the Indian name of the country.

The civilization of all countries began with the tilling of the soil or agriculture, and this was the case too in the old mother colony. It is generally admitted, that no part of the United States possesses greater natural advantages for the production of cereals, vegetables and orchard fruit than the "Old Dominion!" Situated in the most favorable latitude of the temperate zone, with variety of soil and enormous mineral resources, richly watered and with the best harbors on the Atlantic coast, it was well qualified to become the starting point of English colonization. But already in selecting the locality of the first settlement, the English colonists were injudicious by choosing a low and unhealthy section.

Early in 1607 the London Company sent out Captain Christopher Newport, with three small ships, the Susan Constance, the Discoverer and the God-speed, coming with one hundred and five men to establish a colony. Before the departure from England a form of government was prepared and all power was vested in a body of seven councillors, whose names were: Edward Maria Wingfield, president, and Capt. John Smith, Christ. Newport, John Ratcliffe, John Martin, Bartholomew Gosnold and George Kendall. The original intention was to settle on Roanoke Island, but a storm drove the little fleet into the Chesapeake Bay and it sailed up the "Powhatan River" to which the adventurers gave the name of "James." Upon its banks, about fifty miles from its mouth, they established the settlement "Jamestown." Unfortunately most of the settlers were English noblemen and adventurers, not fond of work and even despising it, and therefore, they were but little qualified to do the hard labors of pioneers. "Vagabond gentlemen" as they are called in some American histories for schools,[2 & 3]) they had no families and came in search of wealth, expecting when rich to return to England and to commence anew a life of dissipation. They imported into America nothing but their prejudice and faults, and even President Wingfield soon showed himself a heartless scoundrel. Not much good could be expected of such elements for the new colony.

---

2) "American History for Schools," by G. P. Quackenbos, p. 43. New York, 1877.

3) "History of the United States of America," by Ch A. Goodrich and W. Seavy, p. 31. N. Y. 1867.

Mr. Cooke[4]) who lived in Virginia on the old homestead of his ancestors and who took an earnest interest in the history of his native State, describes the precaution with which the ships of the daring seamen approached the coast and the landing of Newport's expedition as follows:

Before them was the great expanse of Chesapeake Bay, the "Mother of waters" as the Indian name signified, and in the distance the broad mouth of a great river, the Powhatan. As the ships approached the western shore of the bay the storm had spent its force, and they called the place Point Comfort. A little further, at the present Hampton, they landed and were hospitably received by a tribe of Indians. The ships then sailed on up the river, which was new-named James River, and parties landed here and there, looking for a good site for the colony. A very bad one was finally selected, a low peninsula half buried in the tide at highwater. Here the adventurers landed on May 13th, 1607, and gave the place the name of Jamestown, in honor of the King. Nothing remains of this famous settlement but the ruins of a church tower covered with ivy, and some old tombstones. The tower is crumbling year by year, and the roots of trees have cracked the slabs, making great rifts across the names of the old Armigers and Honourables. The place is desolate, with its washing waves and flitting seafowl, but possesses a singular attraction. It is one of the few localities which recall the first years of American history, but it will not recall them much longer. Every distinctive feature of the spot is slowly disappearing. The river encroaches year by year, and the ground occupied by the original huts is already submerged."

Mr. Cooke gives in his pretty description a fair picture of the unfitness of the first immigrants, and also unintentionally shows a characteristic difference between the English and the Germans, that exists to this day. His complaint concerning the unmitigated decay of the mementoes of such an important event, as the first settlement in Virginia was, is fully justified and deserves honorable mentioning, but this demonstrates also how

---

4) "Virginia," A History of the People, by John Esten Cooke, p. 19. Boston, Mass., 1883.

irreverent and little ideal the Anglo-Americans are in such matters in contrast with the Germans, who perhaps less smart and enterprising in the practices of life are of deeper feeling and reverence. Not until 1891 were the first steps taken to preserve the few remaining ruins of old Jamestown to posterity. Congress appropriated ten thousand dollars to prevent the further destruction of the island, and an embankment with ripraps has been built along the northern end, but the work is badly done, and already the bank is beginning to be undermined. Like "red tape" this characteristic difference between the two principal elements of the population is to be observed in the history of the Union and particularly of Virginia.

It is also not to be left unmentioned, that *the oldest printed publication* about Virginia is a German one. A chronological list of works up to Capt. Smith's death, 1631, published in "The English Scholar's Library," Birmingham, 1884, page cxxxii, names in the very first place: "1590–1650 Levinius Hulsius, A Collection of Voyages. In German-Frankfort." Furthermore, on page cxxxiv is stated, "In 1617, Hulsius, the German collector, translated Smith's description for his voyages and reengraved the map (drawn by Captain Smith); but the names in the lower corners were omitted, and Smith's title, the verses concerning him and some of the explanations were given in German. In regard to Capt. Smith's map, printed by Georg Low in London, is said in the same publication, "The original condition of the map bears in the lower left-hand corner, Simon Pasacus, sculpit," which appears to be a latinized German name.

Upon the banks of James river the colonists met with peaceable and hospitable Indians. Powhatan, the chief of the native confederacy, resided at Werowocomoco on the shores of York River. In the beginning friendly relations existed between the colonists and the savages, and Captains Newport and Smith in exploring the country up the James River and eastward to York River, frequently visited the kind-hearted chief in his wigwam. Capt. Smith[5]) reports also, " the savages often visited us kindly."

5.) "The Three Travels." Adventures and Observations of Capt. John Smith. Vol. I, p. 151. London edition, 1629, and republished at Richmond, Va., 1819.

In June 1607 Captain Newport sailed for England, leaving the smallest of his ships behind him and soon the colonists began to experience a variety of calamities. They were, as has already been stated, poorly fitted to struggle with life in the wilderness, neglecting to cultivate the soil and wasting their time in unsuccessful searches for gold. Among them, as stated in Capt. Smith's reports to the London Company, were only four carpenters and twelve laborers,[6]) and most of them were "Dutchmen."

A list of the "first planters" gives the following probably anglicized names of the four carpenters: William Laxon, Edward Pising, Thomas Emry and Robert Small, and in 1609, Adam and Francis, two stout Dutchmen, are mentioned. No distinction was made in those days between the appellations "Dutch" and "Deutsch or German." Germans and Hollanders came to England and America by way of the same Dutch harbors. However, Capt. John Smith, speaking of the natives of Holland in his "Description of New England," always calls them Hollanders *and not Dutch*. From a recommendation to the Council of Virginia[7]): "To send *to Germany* and Poland for laborers," it can safely be concluded, *that those carpenters and laborers were Germans, and that they have built the first dwelling houses in Virginia.* This conjecture appears the more plausible, as the other immigrants were not skilled to this work. Furthermore Capt. Smith had travelled through Poland *and Germany* and knew the Germans as an industrious and reliable people. He also ordered three of his "German" carpenters as he distinctly calls them and as will be further related, to build a house for the Indian Chief Powhatan, and that he made great efforts to persuade them to return, when they preferred to remain with the natives.

In "Hening's Statutes at Large," Vol. I, p. 114–118; dated July 24th, 1621, instructions drawn up by the Council, also refer to the care to be taken of Frenchmen, Dutch, Italians and others, and clearly indicate the presence of emigrants from various nations.

6.) "The English Scholar's Library." pp. 94 and 130. Birmingham, 1894; and "Historical Collections of Virginia," by Henry Howe, p. 24. Charleston, S. C., 1819.

7.) "The English Scholar's Library," pp. 194, 195, 196, 197, 444 &c. Birmingham, 1884; and "The Three Travels," by Capt. John Smith. Vol. I, p. 202. Richmond, Va., 1819.

The documents giving the names of the first comers are incomplete, but contain a number of German family names. In the letter to the Council, before mentioned, Capt. John Smith speaks with distinction of one *Capitaine Richard Waldo* and a *Maister Andrew Buckler*. The lists of the arrivals from 1607 to 1609, expressly confirm the presence of Dutch and Poles[8]) and contain the following names of German sound: *John Herd, Henry Leigh, Thomas Lavander, William, George* and *Thom. Cassen, Wm. Unger, Wm. May, Vere, Michaell, Peter Keffer,* a gunner, *Wm. Dowman, Thomas Feld,* apothecary, *Rose, Milman, Michaell Lowicke, Hillard, Nath. Graues,* (probably *Krause,*) etc. In a list of the names of the adventurers of Virginia, contained in a printed book edited by the treasurer and Council in 1620,[9]) we meet also with names of German sound as, *David Borne, Wm. Beck, Benjamin Brand, Charles Beck, George Bache, J. Ferne, J. Fenner, L. Campe, Abraham Colmer, John Francklin, Peter Franck, J. Geering, G. Holeman, J. Heiden, G. Herst, N. Hide, J. Harper, Christ. Landman, John Landman, H. Leigh, H. May, J. Miller, J. Martin, J. Mundz, Rich. Morer, Rich. Paulson, N. Salter, A. Speckhard, Henry Spranger, Dr. Wm. Turner, Rich. Turner, J. Treuer, J. Tauerner, R. and H. Venne, J. Weld, John Waller* and many doubtful names.

Provisions were scarce and of poor quality, sickness spread among the settlers, and before the beginning of winter 1607 one half had perished. Worse than all these misfortunes, the neighboring Indians, alarmed by the intrusion and unkind treatment of the whites, became jealous and hostile and refused to furnish supplies of corn, etc.

Fortunately in this desperate position Capt. Smith proved to be the right kind of man to meet the emergency and so deserves the predicate given to him, "the father of Virginia." He succeeded to quiet the savages, to persuade them to provide his starving followers with provisions and thereby saved the rest of the colonists from certain starvation.

However, upon his return to Jamestown, he discovered that President Wingfield was about to leave the colony with some of

8.) "The English Scholar's Library," pp. 108, 120 and 446. Birmingham, 1884; and "The Three Travels." Adventures and Observations of Capt. John Smith. Vol. I, pp. 153, 172, 173, 181, 203 and 205, from London edition of 1629, republished at Richmond, Va., 1819.

9) The Generall Historie of Virginia" etc , by Capt. John Smith. Vol. II, pp. 43 – 56. Richmond, Va., 1819.

his partisans and the most valuable stores on Capt. Newport's ship bound for the West Indies. He forced the treacherous President to stay, and Wingfield being disposed of, Capt. Smith was appointed to his office and restored order. He trained his English companions to swinging the axe in the woods and to till the soil, declaring that, "he who would not work, should not eat."

Soon new troubles arose with the Indians and Capt. Smith planned with *Capitaine Waldo*, (this name indicates that the Captain was a German or German descendant,) "upon whom he knew he could rely in time of need,"[10]) to subdue them. Not being very conscientious in regard to the means for accomplishing his design, he resolved to lurk the unsuspecting Powhatan into his power. In one of his reports he mentions, that he proposed to the Indian chief to erect for him a dwelling house after the European pattern and that he ordered three of his *German carpenters* and two Englishmen, "having so small allowance and few were able to do anything to purpose,"[11]) to do the job. He instructed these artisans to act also as spies and assist him to accomplish his object to get the Indian chief in his power. But the Germans learned to esteem the Indians and particularly the well meaning Powhatan, and finally they gave warning to the chief and resolved to stay and live with the sons of the wilderness. It seems that these men had endured many privations amidst the English, for Capt. Smith says, "it would have done well, but to send them and without victualls to work, was not so well advised nor considered of, as it should have been."[12]) When Capt. Smith heard of this socalled treachery of the German workmen, he angrily remarked as "Fama" reports, "damned Dutch," and accordingly he ought to be looked upon as the author of the illbred predicate which is to this day in use by ill meaning people. Wherever different nationalities are mixed together, there will be some rivalry, and American life illustrates this fact from Capt. Smith's time to the present. It seems too, from the captain's statements, that the

---

10.) "The Three Travels." Adventures and Observations of Capt John Smith Vol I, p. 204, from the London edition, 1629, and republished at Richmond, Va., 1819; and "The English Scholar's Library," pp. 130 and 447. Birmingham, 1884.

11.) Do. Vol. I, p. 205.

12.) Do. Vol. I, p. 193; and "The English Scholar's Library," p. 122. Birmingham, 1884.

" Dutchmen " had ·" English " confederates[13]) and it is well known, that dissatisfaction and discord split the colonists in adverse parties.

The intrigue of Capt. Smith reawakened the suspicion of the natives, and the bad feeling was increased to bitter hatred by the following occurrence. The Indians[14]) had raised an abundant harvest, but to secure a portion of it was no easy task for the colonists. Smith, however, determined to undertake it and in company with five companions he descended the James as far as Hampton Roads, where he landed, and went boldly among the savages, offering to exchange hatchets and coin for corn, but they only laughed at the proposal and mocked the strangers by offering a piece of bread for Smith's sword and musket. Smith, always determined to succeed in every undertaking, abandoned the idea of barter and resolved to fight. He ordered his men to fire upon the unarmed natives, who ran howling into the woods, leaving their wigwams, filled with corn, an easy prey of the English, but not a grain was touched until the Indians returned. In a short time sixty or seventy painted warriors, at the head of whom marched a priest bearing an idol, appeared and made an attack. The English gave fire a second time, made a rush, drove the savages back and captured their idol. The Indians, when they saw their deity in possession of the English, sent the priest to humbly beg for its return. Smith stood with his musket across the prostrate image and dictated the only terms upon which he would surrender it; that six unarmed Indians should come forward and fill his boat with corn. The terms were accepted, the idol given up, and Smith returned to Jamestown with a boat load of supplies, but leaving behind him enraged enemies.

Capt. Smith soon afterwards made several trips of exploration, thinking it possible to discover a passage to the Pacific. On one of these expeditions, while sailing up the Chickahominy river, he was attacked by a party of Indians and taken prisoner. His captors carried him before their chief Powhatan and after a long consultation he was condemned to die. The executioners rushed forward and dragged their victim to a large stone on which it

---

13) "The Three Travels." Adventures and Observations of Capt. John Smith. Vol. I, p. 218, from the London edition, 1629, republished at Richmond, Va., 1819.

14) "History of West Virginia," by Virgil A Lewis, p. 29 Philadelphia, 1889.

had been decided his head should be crushed. His head already rested on the stone, still shown at the old Mayo farm near Richmond, and the two warriors had raised the club to strike the fatal blow, when Pocahontas, the favorite daughter of the chief, threw herself upon the captive and implored her father to spare the life of the prisoner. Powhatan yielded to the maiden's prayer. Smith was released and in a few days concluded a bargain with the old chief, by which he was to receive a large tract of country in exchange for two cannon and a grindstone, which were to be sent from Jamestown. Accompanied by a guard of twelve men he arrived there after an absence of seven weeks, and under the pretext of instructing the Indian guardsmen in the use of the cannons, discharged them into the trees, at which the savages were so frightened, that they would have nothing to do with them. The grindstone proved so heavy, that they could not carry it, and finally they returned with only a number of trinkets.

Pocahontas, a girl of thirteen years of age, loved the captain dearly. She afterwards embraced the Christian faith and was baptized Rebecca. After the return of Smith to England in 1609, a young English settler, John Rolfe, assured her that Smith died and persuaded her to marry him. Three years later the couple visited England and she was received with great ceremony at the royal court. There she met with Captain Smith and it is said, that she died heart broken finding herself the victim of deceit. She left one son, who was educated in England and who then returned to Virginia, where several of the most prominent families claim to be his descendants.

The poetical Pocahontas tale has been related here in full, to prove the correctness of the assertion made previously in regard to the lack of devotion to the memoirs of history on part of Anglo-Americans. No prominent American poet has taken hold of this admirable story, but the German-American teacher, Johann Straubenmueller, published in German in 1858 at Baltimore, Md., a poem entitled: "Pocahontas or the foundation of Virginia." It is an astonishing fact, that more German-American, and even German poets, as for instance, Friedrich von Schiller[15] and Nicolaus Lenau,[16] have selected American

---

15) „Nadowessier's Todtenlied," by Friedrich von Schiller.
16.) „Der Indianerzug," „Die drei Indianer," etc., by Nicolaus Lenau.

myths and Indian life for their poetry and saved those precious pearls from falling into oblivion, than native American poets. The original painting of Pocahontas, a picture which has long been sought for and which is now ascertained to be in Norfolk, is probably too the work of a German artist, Nicolaus Locker.[17])

After friendly relations were again reestablished between Smith and Powhatan, the captain tried to induce the German carpenters sent to the Indian chief to return to Jamestown. He granted them full pardon and detailed a Swiss, by name William Volday, to persuade them, but his messenger also preferred to stay with the Indians and only one German, named *Adam*, availed himself of the captain's offer.[18]) Capt. Smith then charged the Dutchmen, — or the cursed country-men of the Swiss Volda or Volday, as he called them, — to have conspired with the Spaniards to destroy the colony. In an interesting historical publication, "Die unbekannte neue Welt oder Beschreibung des Welttheils Amerika, by Dr. O. D., Amsterdam, 1673," of which a copy is in possession of Rev. Eduard Huber, Baltimore, Md., the unwise and oppressive treatment the Germans suffered by the English and their consequent enmity, is confirmed. On page 161 of this Dutch book is stated, "They (the Englishmen) had also many troubles with the High-Germans (Hochdeutschen,) which having been badly treated, joined the Virginians (the Indians) to destroy the English settlement." Thus it appears, that the grievances experienced, induced the German colonists to actions of a hostile character and that in those early days of the colony a want of harmony created a deplorable national calamity, which has continued in some degree to this day.

Being unable to induce the German mechanics to return to Jamestown, Capt. Smith persuaded Thomas Douse and Thomas Mallard "to bring the Dutchmen and the inconstant savages in such a manner amongst such ambuscades, as he had prepared, that not many of them should return from the peninsula."[19]) But Douse failed to accomplish his design.

17) "The English Scholar's Library," page 136. Birmingham, 1884.

18) "The Three Travels." Adventures and Observations by Capt. John Smith Vol I, pp. 231, 232. Richmond, Va., 1819.

19.) "The English Scholar's Library," page 477. Birmingham, 1884.

In the spring and again in the fall of 1608 Capt. Newport arrived with provisions and new immigrants. Among the newcomers were a number of Poles and Germans, brought over with the purpose to manufacture pitch, tar, glass, sope-ashes, etc., but most of the new settlers were of the same sort as their predecessors, who in spite of the remonstrances of Smith, wasted their time in search of gold. Capt. Smith complained of the habits and character of the men sent out and entreated the council, "when they send out again, rather to send but thirty carpenters, husbandmen, gardeners, fishermen, blacksmiths, masons and diggers of tree roots, well provided, than a thousand of such as they had." The bad state of affairs continued and after two years of existence, there were but forty acres of cultivated land in the colony.

In the year 1609 the London Company obtained a new charter, granting enlarged territory and putting the management of affairs of the colony in the hands of a governor assisted by a council. Lord Delaware was appointed governor, after Capt. Smith, by the accidental explosion of a bag of gunpowder, had been wounded and obliged to return to England. Besides Jamestown, that was strongly palisaded, containing some fifty or sixty houses, he left five or six other forts and plantations. It was an unlucky day for the colony when Capt. Smith departed, — his actions had not always been free of harshness and cruelty, — but the circumstances that surrounded him may serve for his excuse, — and when he had left, disorder, sickness and famine ensued. The winter of 1609 to 1610 was properly termed "the starving time." Of the 490 persons whom Smith left, only sixty survived, and it may safely be accepted, that most of the survivors belonged to the industrious, sober working class from the European continent, while the English fortune seekers, carrying on a dissipate life, perished. Capt. Smith stated,[20] "the adventurers never knew what a day's work was, except the Dutchmen and Poles, and some dozen others. For all the rest were poor gentlemen, tradesmen, serving men, libertines and such like, ten times more fit to spoil a commonwealth, than either begin one, or but help to maintain one."

---

[20] "The Three Travels." Adventures and Observations. Vol. I, p. 241. Richmond, 1819.

The Indians, no longer afraid, began to harass the unfortunates, who concluded to desert the settlement and to sail to Newfoundland. Nearing the mouth of the James river, they descried a fleet entering Hampdon roads. It was Lord Delaware with new colonists and provisions, and the disheartened fugitives were persuaded to return to the abandoned Jamestown. The new arrivals were of a better class and by the judicious management of the governor the future of the colony wore a brighter aspect.

Among the new settlers were many Dutch and Germans, they plowed the soil, corn was raised in abundance and no further famine again endangered the lives of the colonists. Tobacco and cotton were extensively cultivated for export, and tobacco was used as money, being worth about 75 cents a pound. Capt. Waldo, before mentioned and highly esteemed by Capt. Smith, went to England and persuaded the merchants to commence mining in Virginia. But the mines he had found did not prove rich and he was treated as an impostor and died most miserably.[21] The remains of an iron furnace[22] are found in Chesterfield County, five or six miles below Richmond, described by Berkeley in his History of Virginia as being worked in 1620. Very likely these iron works were established by Capt. Waldo. In the Price-Lists of 1621 iron is marked at twelve pounds sterling per ton, but in 1622 the Chesterfield furnace was broken up by the massacre of the Indians under the chief Opechancanough.

Ill health soon obliged governor Delaware to give up the administration of the colony and he was succeeded by Sir Thomas Dale. The last act of governor Dale marks an era in the history of Virginia. Ever since the foundation of the colony all property was held in common, the settlers worked together and the products of the harvest were deposited in a common storehouse and distributed by the council. Governor Dale now introduced the policy of assigning to each settler a few acres of land to be his own, and the advantages of this system soon became apparent in the general improvement.

21) "The Three Travels." Adventures and Observations. Vol. I, p 241. Richmond, 1819.

22.) "The Hand-Book of Virginia," p. 64 Fifth Edition Richmond, Va , 1886.

In the year 1611 the colony counted 200 inhabitants and the settlements extended on both sides of the James. In several of the reports to the London Company the presence of Germans is confirmed and they show, that the administration appreciated diligent labor and endeavored to encourage immigration from France, Germany, Switzerland, and Holland. The intolerance of the clergy and of the worldly rulers in Europe furthered the realization of this plan.

Before 1619 the colonists had no part in the making of the laws by which they were governed, but in that year, under the administration of Sir George Yeardley, a representative government was established, and in order to further ensure the permanency of the colony through the establishment of family life, one hundred and fifty agreeable young women, poor but respectable, were brought over. They were sold to the planters in marriage bound at the cost of their transportation expenses, at the price of one hundred pounds of tobacco, and the demand exceeding the supply, other transports were furnished and the price advanced to 150 pounds. This almost comic transaction proved of the highest merit, as domestic and moral life was its result and even the restless adventurers relinquished the fondled hope of returning to the mother land.

It is very probable that many of the German settlers married English women and thereby became anglicized.

Acquisitions of a different and decidedly unfavorable character were also made to the population of the colony. One hundred criminals were, by the order of King James, sent over to be sold for a term of years as servants to the planters, and this beginning created a desire on part of some of the colonists to employ labor and the opportunity to gratify it came only too soon.

In 1620 a Dutch ship from Africa touched at Jamestown and landed twenty negroes, who were sold for lifetime as slaves, and thus the abominable institution of slavery was introduced, spreading gradually over the entire territory of the English colonies — and it became the curse of the inhabitants. In the beginning slavery was only silently tolerated, but in the course of time slave holding, slave breeding and slave trade were protected by law. However, the great majority of the colonists were opposed to the institution and especially to the importation of negroes, and only through the influence of the large land-owners, mostly English lords, was slavery forced on Virginia. Twenty-three statutes were passed by the House of Burgesses *to prevent the importation of slaves,* but all were vetoed by the English government. The general education was purposely neglected and even from the pulpit slavery was declared to be a divine institution.[23]) The Church was urged to keep the mass of the people in a state of ignorance, for fear, that with the progress of intellect the right of humanity might be recognized. Sir William Berkeley, who was appointed governor in 1641, said in the year 1671 in a report to the English government, "I thank God there are no free-schools or printing, for learning has brought disobedience and heresy and sects into the world, and printing has divulged them and libels against the best government. God keep us from both!"—And in fact, not until 1736 was the first newspaper published in Virginia.[24]) In 1730 a prohibitory law was issued, forbidding the German printer *John Buckner,* who had set up *the first printing press* in the mother colony, to publish in print the laws of the government." A school law was not passed by the Assembly until 1796, and it was never carried out. 'In 1818 and 1846 additional laws were passed, but unfortunately,[25]) as in the case of the law of 1796, it was left optional with the counties to adopt or reject it, and the result was a failure to secure any State system. The census of 1860 showed only 85,443 pupils in 3778 schools, so-called, though many were but private classes in which some public fund pupils were instructed. Not until the year 1870 was the present excellent public school law inaugurated in Virginia and at once the enrolment showed for that year 157,841 pupils in all schools, — an immense advance on any previous year.

Slave holding also had most injurious effects on the development of industry and commerce. As long as the mass of a people is without an own income, — as long as all the pro-

23) "Geschichte der deutschen Schulbestrebungen in Amerika," by Herrmann Schuricht, p 4. Leipzig, 1884.

24) Compare, "History of Printing," by Thomas.

25.) Report of the Commissioner of Education for 1876, p 401. Washington, government printing office, 1878.

ducts of the soil are the property of a few, — there is no market except for farm produce and no exchange for surplus. This is shown by statistics. Of imports, the share of the South as compared with the free states before the war of secession, was like 40 to 321, and this proves, that a very small portion of the southern commerce was in southern hands. There certainly would have been tenfold more commerce and manufacture in Virginia and the other southern states, if there had been intelligent, industrious and patriotic free laborers, receiving pay for their work and spending their money for the necessaries and luxuries of life. But for slavery, Virginia would to-day be, as it was in 1790, the most populous state of the Union, as well as the most wealthy and influential. Slavery still had another disastrous effect, — it has the tendency to degrade free labor and to render the free laborer worthless. The habit of giving preference to slave-labor has operated to the prejudice of free labor. It has caused the population of little means to grow up in idleness, to think labor degrading, to be incapable of earnest regular work, and it kept away immigration of white workingmen, because they disliked to be looked down upon and treated as negroes.

The German settlers, whose number was much larger than is generally conceded, were with very few exceptions opposed to slavery, — resulting to their great disadvantage. The slaveholders consequently distrusted the Germans and a new feeling of animosity towards them sprang up. Their political influence was curtailed, and the majority of them submitted in order to secure toleration and peace. In this way a valuable civil element was almost excluded from building up the future state, — but only in political respects and not in its social and economical life. In farming and in commerce the Germans became important factors, as will be shown hereafter. But outside of slavery there was another obstacle in the path of quick development of the colony, that impeded foreign and particularly German immigration.

"The feudal system," says Mr. Ben. Perley Poor,[26]) "was transplanted to Virginia from England and the royal grants of

---

26.) "History of Agriculture of the United States," by Ben. Perley Poor, U. S. Agricultural Report of 1866, p. 505.

land gave the proprietors, — mostly favorites of the King, — baronial power. One of these grants or "patents," as they were called, gave the patentee the right to divide the said tract or territory of land into counties, hundreds, parishes, tithings, townships, hamlets and boroughs, and to erect and build cities, towns, etc., and to endow the same at their free will and pleasure, and did appoint them full and perpetual patrons of all churches, with power also to divide a part or parcel of said tract or territory, or portion of land, into manors and to call the same after their own or any of their names, or by other name or names whatsoever; and within the same to hold court in the nature of a court baron, and to hold pleas of all actions, trespasses, covenants, accounts, contracts, detinues, debts, and demands whatsoever when the debt or thing demanded exceed not the value of forty shilling, sterling money of England, and to receive and take all amercements, fruits, commodities, advantages, perquisites and emoluments whatsoever, to such respective court barons belonging or in any wise appertaining and further, to hold within the same manors a court lect and view of frank pledge of all the tenants, residents and inhabitants of the hundred within such respective manors, etc."

The power being thus vested in the hands of a few lords, desirable immigrants did not come in large numbers as had been expected. Convicts and a great many indentured white servants, Irish and Scotch prisoners of war, were sent over from England in and after the year 1621, — but after a generation or two all these elements became blended into a homogeneous mass of "cavaliers,"— aristocratic because they had an inferior race beneath them.

Still, in spite of all the mismanagement and unlucky circumstances, the colony extended its lines and soon after immigration began to penetrate into the interior.

Until the death of Powhatan in 1618 the settlers lived fairly in peace with the natives, but after his brother Opechancanough (speak Ope-kan-kano) became the head of the confederate tribes, the relations changed. Eyeing with suspicion the increasing numbers of the palefaces, he laid a murderous plan in 1622 for their total extermination.

Mr. Virgil A. Lewis[27]) describes the cruel massacre, which
also caused the death of many a German settler, as follows:
"In order to avoid suspicion, he, Opechancanough, renewed the
treaty of peace with governor Wyatt, and only two days before
the blow was to be struck he declared that the sky should fall
before he would violate the terms of the treaty. The friendly
relations were continued up to the very day, even to the fatal
hour. They borrowed boats from the English, brought in veni-
son and other provisions for sale and sat down to breakfast with
their unsuspecting victims. The hour arrived. It was twelve
o'clock noon on the 22nd day of March, 1622, when every hamlet
in Virginia was attacked by a band of yelling savages, who
spared neither age, sex nor condition. The bloody work went
on until 347 men, women and children had fallen victims at the
barbarous hands of that perfidious and inhuman people." The
"Colonial Records of Virginia," published by order of the Sen-
ate, Richmond, Va., 1874, contain a list of all those that were
massacred by the savages, and this document gives the following
names of Germans, besides a very large number of doubtful
names, but of probably German origin: *Robert Horner, Samuel
Stringer, Georg Soldan, Th. Freeman, Edw. Heyden, Edw. Lis-
ter, John Benner, Thomas Sheffeld* and *Robert Walden.*

Had not a converted Indian, who lived with a man named
Pace, revealed the plot and so put the people of Jamestown and
neighboring settlements on their guard, and therefore in a state
of defence, every settlement would have been laid in ruins and
the inhabitants put to the tomahawk. So the plan failed. There
were yet 1600 fighting men in the colony and the Indians were
made to pay dear for their perfidy. The English pushed into
the wilderness, burning wigwams, killing every Indian that fell
into their hands, and destroying the crops, until the foe was
driven far into the interior. Confidence was once more restored,
and a feeling of security brought a return of prosperity; immigration revived and at the end of the year the population num-
bered 2500."

Especially one class of the English immigrants caused the
dissatisfaction and provocation of the natives, namely the *pio-*

27.) "History of West Virginia," by Virgil A. Lewis, pp. 46, 47. Phila, Pa., 1889.

neers, who strongly contrasted with the cavalier planters and the regular settlers.[28]) Generally speaking, they were the younger sons, unlucky gamesters, turbulent spirits, rejected lovers and disbanded soldiers, who turned their backs on civilization to live an untrammeled life in some fertile mountain gap or rich river bottom. Game was plentiful and they were hunters and trappers rather than farmers, sending their peltries to market and only cultivating enough land to supply their immediate wants. This unrestrained life became a passion and frequently led to conflicts with the Indians, who claimed the forests as their hunting ground, — and the peaceful and active farmers on the frontier, mostly Germans, suffered much on this account.

The London Company had not gained any profit by the colonization of Virginia so far. She had sent over more than 9000 persons at an expense of about 100,000 pounds sterling, — many of the immigrants perished, others had joined the Indians or left the country, — and after eighteen years of existence the colony counted only 2500 inhabitants, and the annual export scarcely amounted to 20,000 pounds.

King James too was little pleased with these meagre results, and when the Indian troubles commenced and the very existence of the colony was endangered, he dissolved the company and in 1624 Virginia was declared a royal province. The Colonial Assembly was however allowed to exercise its former power, and by and by the importance of Virginia was felt. A thousand immigrants arrived in the single year 1627 and took to farming whereever fertile land invited them.

The "Colonial Records of Virginia" contain lists of the living and dead in Virginia on Feb. 16th, 1623, that give the following German names: *William Welder, Margaret Berman, Henry Coltman, Mrs. Coltman, Petters, Richard Spurling (Sperling), John Landman, Daniel Vergo, Wm. Boocke, Walter Priest, Henry Turner, Edw. Bricke, Elizabeth Salter, Ch. Waller, Georg Graues, Th. Spilman, Th. Rees, John Rose, Wm. Stocker, Wm. Kemp, George Fryer, Peter Staber, John Filmer, John Rachell* and *Margarett Pollentin, Adam Rumell, Nicholas Wesell, John Salter, Cornelius* and *Elizabeth May* and child, *Wm. Cappe, Peter*

---

28) "History of the Agriculture of the United States," by Ben. Perley Poor, Agricultural Report of the U. S., p. 506, Washington, 1867.

Longman, Robert Winter, Richard Spriese, Sam. Foreman, Daniel Francke, Rich. Ranke, Vallentyne Gentler, Th. Horner, Cathrin Cappe and a very large number of doubtful names.

Tobacco had become the staple product of Virginia and efforts were made to also encourage other branches of rural industry. Cotton was first planted in 1621 and its cultivation was now promoted. King James I, prompted doubtless by his antipathy to "the Virginia weed," as he termed the tobacco plant, and having understood that the soil naturally yielded store of excellent mulberries, gave directions to urge the cultivation of silk and to erect silk-mills. Men of experience were brought over from France, Switzerland and Germany, and premiums were offered to encourage the raising of the silk-worm, and later also that of indigo, hops and other agricultural staples; but fresh disturbances interfered.

The war with the Indians just ended, the political and religious troubles in England, the immorality of the royal court, the corruption of the office holders, the animosity of the tories and wighs, the contest between the church and its opponents, and finally the establishment of a republican government by Cromwell, exercised their convulsive influences even upon distant Virginia.

After the restoration of Charles II to the throne of his beheaded father, he failed to fulfill the expectations of his people, who were in hope that the king, who had gone through a school of misfortune, would give his country peace and prosperity. But Charles II soon lost the confidence and respect of his subjects. He was incapable of resolute action and self-sacrifice, without trust in humanity or virtue. "He was a drunkard, a libertine, and a hypocrite, who had neither shame nor sensibility and who in point of honor was unworthy to enter the presence of the meanest of his subjects."[29])

To have the throne occupied for a quarter of century by such a man as this one, was the surest way of weakening that ignorant and indiscriminate loyalty to which various people have often sacrificed their dearest rights, and to shake the faith in the

29) "History of Civilization in England ," by Henry Thomas Buckle. Vol. I, p. 280. New York, 1870.

continuance of public welfare. Charles II deceived the Protestants by favoring the Catholics, and he rushed England into unlucky wars. He wounded the national pride of his people by the sale of Duenkirchen to Louis XIV of France, and by the defeat in the war with Holland. England, which had advanced during the republican administration to the first naval power of Europe, had to endure the mortification, that a Dutch fleet under de Ruyter sailed up the Thames and alarmed the city of London by the thunder of its cannon. In the treaty of Dorn Charles II agreed to adopt the Catholic faith and to support the claim of the King of France on the Spanish throne with his fleet and army, while on the other hand Louis XIV obliged himself to pay subsidies and to land an army in England in case of revolution. Henry Thomas Buckle says,[30] "Politically and morally there were to be found in the government all the elements of confusion, of weakness and of crime. The king himself was a mean and spiritless voluptuary, without the morals of a Christian and almost without the feeling of man. His ministers had not one of the attributes of statesmen and nearly all of them were pensioned by the crown of France."

The English possessed a great deal of national self-esteem and all the disgrace that the king brought over Great Britain wounded them deeply. The same effect was visible in the English colonies and finally resulted in outbursts of indignation. This was particularly the case in Virginia, where a great number of disgusted English and Scotch refugees had settled, while the immigrants from the European continent possessed no special attachment to the English throne and advocated American independence. The rights of the mass of the colonists were everywhere restricted. Sir William Berkeley, who had held the office of governor by the will of the people, and who had administered the colonial affairs in a liberal manner, was confirmed by Charles II in 1660, but thereupon commenced a rule of despotism and oppression, — the affairs of the Church were placed in the hands of vestries, — and the Assembly composed of aristocrats made themselves permanent. Prospects grew dark !

---

30) "History of Civilization in England," by Henry Thomas Buckle. Vol I, p 275. New York, 1870.

During the time of the Commonwealth in the year 1651, Parliament had extended its authority to America, and in an act required all the exports from the colonies to England to be carried in English or colonial vessels. Virginia expected after the Restoration, in acknowledgment of her loyalty, some special marks of the king's favor, but by compulsory laws, as the above mentioned, she was required to look to England as her sole market for her exports and to receive from England alone her imports. In 1672 duties were even imposed upon articles carried from one colony to another, and these aggressions drove the colonists finally to insurrection.

But the great natural wealth of the land assisted, in spite of restrictions and obstructions, the progress of Virginia. Among the various strange and surprising things which the settlers found on Virginian soil, were a great variety of wild grape vines, and the London Company determined, as early as 1630, to make some experiments with the culture of the European canes through French and German experts. The favorite drinks of the English were, at that time: portwine, sherry and madeira, and it is easy to understand, that they desired to produce wines of this character in Virginia. Premiums were offered to encourage the cultivation of vines, but the delicate European sorts did not resist the injuries of climate and insects, and the results were unsatisfactory.

At about the same time a German-Bohemian named *Augustine Herrmann*, from Prague in Bohemia, came to Virginia.[31]) His name is mentioned also with distinction in the annals of other North-American colonies, as, New Amsterdam, now New York,—New Jersey and Maryland, and in fact the Dutch colonies are principally entitled to claim him as theirs, but his services in regard to Virginia are of such great merit, that his name ought for all time to be given a place of honor in her history.

There is very little known about the early life of Herrmann, — even the year of his birth is only judged to be 1605. It seems that he came to Virginia in 1629, for in a petition addressed to the Dutch governor Stuyvesant, dated 1654, he says: "Without

---

31) "Deutsch-Amerikanisches Magazin," H. A. Rattermann. Numbers 2 and 4. Cincinnati, O., 1886.

specially praising myself, *I am the founder of the Virginia tobacco trade,* and it is well known that in a short time great advantages for the public welfare have been called forth thereby."
This assertion of Herrmann has never been controverted, and as
a memorial of the deputies of the Dutch West India Company,
dated November 16th, 1629, speaks of "a large quantity of tobacco, which now has become an important article of trade,[32])
it may safely be accepted that the above statement in respect to
the time of his arrival in Virginia is correct.

Later Herrmann removed to New Amsterdam and began
business of his own and as agent for Peter Gabry & Co., Amsterdam. He was also a wholesale dealer in wine, bought and sold
furs, Virginia cotton and tobacco, which he exported to Holland.
It is proved by documents that he received the last named articles, by the intervention of *Georg Hack* in Northampton, Va.,
whose wife was a sister of Mrs. Herrmann, né Jeanetie Verlet,
from Utrecht, and who frequently visited her relatives in New
Amsterdam. In exchange for Virginia products Herrmann sup-
plied his brother-in-law with all kinds of imported goods.

Georg Hack apparently was a man of energy and influence,
who took an active part in politics. He was one of the sub-
scribers to the so-called "engagement of Northampton,"[33]) dated
March 25th, 1651, by which the county declared itself in favor of
Parliament, respectively of Cromwell and the republic. This action of Hack deserves special mention, as most Virginians were
at that crisis loyal royalists and bitterly opposed the "Navigation
Act" enforced by the British Parliament. This law, as has been
stated, prohibited export and import except to and from England and was necessarily a severe blow to the foreign trade established by Hack's brother-in-law. Georg Hack appears therefore as a man of character, who would rather sacrifice the interests of his relative and his own, than depart from his principles.

Herrmann on the other hand defended the interests of the
Dutch with energy and soon gained respect and influence.
Several times during the period of the Commonwealth, he was

---

32) L. van Aitzema, "Historie van Saken van Staet en Oorlogh, in ende omtrent de
Vereen Nederland, etc." 4° edition Vol. II, p. 912. An English translation is to be found
in: "Documents relating to the colonial history of New York." Vol. I, pp. 40—42.

33.) "Virginia Historical Register." Vol. I, p. 163.

sent as ambassador by governor Stuyvesant to Virginia and Maryland, and his reports are still preserved in the state archive of New York at Albany.[34])

Besides his creditable doings as merchant and statesman, he gained fame in another way. He advocated, as early as 1659, in a letter to governor Stuyvesant: an accurate geographical survey of the English and Dutch colonies,[35]) and he was possessed of the talent and knowledge to undertake the difficult work himself. He was well posted in literature, spoke the most important languages: German, English, Dutch, French, Spanish and Latin, and he was an efficient draughtsman, mathematician and surveyor. Edwin R. Purple calls him[36]) "a man of good education, a surveyor by profession, talented in sketching and a draughtsman, — a smart and enterprising business man, — a rare and noble man, — and an admirer of this country."

Probably the map of the New Netherland, printed by Nicolaus Jan Visscher and contained in von der Donk's book, "Beschreyvings van Nieuw Nederland," published at Amsterdam in 1655, was drawn by Herrmann, as it is certain, that the view of New Amsterdam, which is also contained in the book, originates from him. Beyond all doubt he has drawn in 1670 the "map of the English and Dutch colonies," which was published by the government in 1673 and embraces the section between the line of North Carolina and the Hudson river. Although incorrect in several respects, it gives a very comprehensive picture of the land, mouths of rivers and inlets of the sea. Virginia is particularly well drawn, and Herrmann must have explored the tidewater-region very carefully. The map shows the likeness of its designer with the inscription, "Augustine Herrmann, Bohemian," and a vignette with the inscription, "Virginia and Maryland as it was planted and inhabited this present year 1670. Surveyed and exactly drawn by our own labor and endeavor of Augustine Herrmann, Bohemiensis," and at the side of which are represented a young Indian with bow and arrow, and an Indian girl.

It is of great interest that Herrmann's map also gives some German names of places in Virginia, as: Scharburg and Backer's

34) "Dutch Manuscript." Vol. XVIII, p. 96.
35) "Deutsch-Amerikanisches Magazin." Copy 4, pp. 535 to 536.
36) "The New York Genealogical and Biographical Record." Vol. IX, pp. 57 to 58.

Creek. This is almost proof, that in the very infancy of the colony German settlements existed. Augustine Herrmann died in 1686.

It appears also that Germans occupied high political offices, before and during the governorship of Sir Wm. Berkeley. One *Richard Kempe* was secretary of the land office of Henrico in 1624, member of the council of Virginia in 1642, president of this body in 1644, and during the time Sir Berkeley visited England, *acting governor*. The name Kempe is undoubtedly German, but some historians write him "Kemp," and claim erroneously that this form of the name is English. Yet Kemp, as well as Kempe, are to this day German family names and the land-registers of Henrico of 1624[37]) contain many signatures in Rich. Kempe's own handwriting—and with but one exception he signed "Kempe." Furthermore all biographies of the English colonial governors[38]) give the name of their native land, county and birthplace, with the sole exception of R. Kempe's biography, and this omission also speaks for his German origin. Surely there is no full evidence that R. Kempe was a German, but the probabilities are in favor of it.

During the same period some Germans rendered very valuable services by exploring the unknown country in the interior.

Johannes Lederer was the first explorer of the Alleghany mountains, and he is one of the brightest figures in the early history of the German element in Virginia. The German-American historian H. A. Rattermann, of Cincinnati, O., deserves credit for the preservation of the great deeds of Lederer,[39]) and an extract from his researches may find room at this place.

In the year 1668 Johannes Lederer came to Jamestown and offered his services to governor Berkeley. "A son of the Alps," as he said, "he had come to explore America." He was a scientific man and familiar with several languages, especially the classical, and he expressed the desire to explore the mountain region. Governor Berkeley readily equipped an expedition to

---

37.) "Land Patents No I," preserved in the land office, Capitol Building, Richmond, Va.

38) "Virginia and the Virginians," by Dr. Brook, Secretary of the Historical Society of Virginia.

39.) "Der erste Erforscher des Alleghany Gebirges: Johannes Lederer," by H. A. Rattermann, "Deutscher Pionier." Jahrgang 8. Cincinnati, O., 1876.

accompany him. Lederer undertook three trips, but failed to discover an easy passage through the mountains, which the governor wished for. During his last expedition his companions became disheartened and deserted him, while he ventured to continue his researches with only an Indian guide, who served him as interpreter. At his return he was ill-treated, — his companions, ashamed of their cowardice, circulated false reports about him, — and finding even his life endangered, he fled to Maryland. Sir William Talbot, governor of the colony, received him kindly, and upon his suggestion he wrote an account of his trips in Latin, which was printed in English in London in 1672 with a map of the country drawn by the author. This interesting little book was entitled: "The Discoveries of John Lederer, in Their Several Marches From Virginia to the West of Carolina and Other Parts of the Continent, begun in March, 1669, and Ended in September, 1670, Etc., with Map, London, 1672." and contains 27 pages, 4°. A copy of it is preserved in the library of the U. S. Congress at Washington City. It is the first scientific report about the geology, botany, animals and native tribes of the extensive district as far as Florida, seen by the courageous German, and it deserves special acknowledgment in a German-American history, giving evidence, that the first exploration of the Alleghanies was the work of a German.

Very little is known of Lederer himself and no reports are left of his later career and end. The family name of Lederer is well known in Austria and Germany. At Wittenberg in Prussia, Grossenhain in Saxony, Marburg in Hessia, Vienna and Innsbruck in Austria, etc., several members of this illustrious family occupied high positions. Some Lederers held diplomatic offices in the United States of America. One, Baron Alois Lederer, was Consul General of Austria and Toscana at New York, and his son Carl was ambassador at Washington City in 1868.

Lederer's map, which appeared with his book, gives only an inaccurate picture of the country, but it must be taken in consideration that his instruments had been carried off by his faithless companions. It shows the land from Virginia to Florida.

In those early times maps only gave general outlines, and all parts not explored had to be guesswork. This may be illustrated by the following.

"A Map of Virginia discovered to ye Hills," 1651, gives to the American continent from the southern cape of Delaware to "the sea of China and the East Indies," a width of less than 300 miles. — On Hennepin's map of 1683, Lake Erie extends to the southern line of Virginia, making the entire state of Ohio part of the lake. — A map of Wm. Delisle, published by Joh. Justin Gebauer and affixed to Bruzen la Martinièr's "Introduction à l'histoire de l'Asie, de l'Afrique et de l'Amerique, etc.," Paris, 1735, presents nothing of the Ohio river and places the source of the Wabash near the Erie in Pennsylvania. — More accurate is a map: "Nouvelle France," by Charlevoix, 1743. — The "Carte de la Virginie et du Maryland, dressée sur la grande carte anglaise de Messrs. Josue Fry[40]) and Pierre Jefferson par Robert de Vaugondy, Géographe ordinaire du Roi," 1755, gives a fair picture of the lands along the coast of the Atlantic, but the section on the other side of the Blue Ridge and the Alleghanies is very inaccurately drawn, — and the same may be said in respect to the old map designed by Augustine Herrmann.

Another German explorer of Virginia is mentioned by Klauprecht, the chronicler of the Ohio valley,—by John Esten Cook,—and by Stierlein in his history of Kentucky and the city of Louisville: the German *Capt. Heinrich Batte,* who in 1667 crossed the Alleghanies and reached the Ohio river.

All these historical facts show that the colonial governments have used German scientific men to open the wilderness to civilization, and the history of North Carolina, the neighboring state of the Old Dominion, furnishes further evidence.

In 1663 a German Swiss, *Peter Fabian,* from Bern, accompanied an expedition sent out by the English North Carolina Company. The report of this exploring expedition appeared in London in 1665 and bears the signatures of its leaders: Anthony Long, Wm. Milton and Peter Fabian. The last named was certainly the author of the report and the scientific man of the expedition, as is shown by the estimates of distances in *German*

---

40) Mr. Josue Fry has drawn several maps of North America, and his name — Fry, o Frei, or Frey, — indicates that he was a German or of German descent.

S. Kercheval, the historian of the Shenandoah Valley, says (History of the Valley of Va , Winchester, 1833, p. 81): "There were a mixture of Irish and Germans on Cedar Creel and its vicinity : the *Frys,* Newells, Blackburns, Wilsons, etc., were among the number."

and not in English mileage. The report, for instance, states: "On Friday, the 16th, we heaved anchor by north-west wind and sailed up River Cape-Fair 4 or 5 *German* miles, where we came to anchor at 5 to 7 fathoms."

Before the end of the seventeenth century the administration of the Swiss Canton Bern planned to establish colonies in North America with the surplus of her population. *Franz Ludwig Michel*[41]), — English historians misname him Mitchell, — was sent to Pennsylvania, Virginia and North Carolina, and John Lawson, the first historian of North Carolina, relates in his book: "A new voyage to Carolina, etc.," printed at London, 1709, and published in German by M. Vischer, Hamburg, in 1712, — that he met on his voyage to the Carolinas the German explorer, who was well acquainted with the land and its people.[42]) Michel again came to North Carolina in 1709, accompanied by *Baron Christopher von Grafenried*, of Bern, at the head of 1500 emigrants from Switzerland and the Palatinate, (die Pfalz in Germany), — all of whom were Germans. Many of these people afterwards settled in Virginia, as will be related further on.

Towards the close of the seventeenth and in the beginning of the eighteenth century, under the leadership of Claude Philippe de Richebourg, another numerous immigration of French Huguenots and German Calvinists or Reformists from Elsace and Loraine took place. These newcomers were industrious and pious people and they scattered successively over the tide-water district, middle Virginia and the Shenandoah valley, but most of them settled in the counties of Norfolk, Surry, Powhatan and Prince William. In the Shenandoah valley they met with a numerous German element and these French Huguenots were perfectly Germanized.

In 1671, by issue of the first law of naturalization, immigration was materially supported. This law prescribed that any

41) "Die Deutschen in Nord-Carolina." Historische Skizze von General J. A. Wagener, Charleston, S. C., publicirt in: "Der deutsche Pionier," Jahrgang III, Seite 328 etc. Cincinnati, Ohio, 1871.

42) "Beitrag zur Geschichte der Deutschen in Nord- und Süd-Carolina," von H. A. Rattermann, publicirt in: "Der deutsche Pionier," Jahrgang X, Seite 189. Cincinnati, Ohio, 1878.

foreigner could be naturalized upon application to the Assembly and by taking the oath of allegiance to the King of England, and that thereafter he should be entitled to hold public office, carry on business, own real estate, etc. The first Germans who applied for naturalization papers were *Joseph Mulder, Heinrich Weedich, Thomas Hastmenson, John Peterson* and *Hermann Keldermann* in 1673.

The number of German settlers during the first century of the existence of the colony was, as has been stated, much larger than is commonly admitted, and some Anglo-American historians unfairly ignore or belittle the share the Germans have taken in the development of Virginia, desiring to represent it as an "entirely English colony." But the old mother colony was from the very beginning *in its character cosmopolitan,* only founded by English enterprise. The following investigations will prove how incorrect and devoid statements of such "manufacturers of history" are.

The Land Patents (Registers) at the land office of Virginia, Capitol building, Richmond, Va., name as early as 1624 to 1635, or during the third decade of the colony, besides many doubtful names, the following German ones: Johann Busch, Thomas Spilman (Spielmann), John Choohman (Schumann), Ph. Clauss, Zacharias Crippe, Christopher Windmill (Windmueller), Henry Coleman (Kohlmann or Kuhlmann), John Loûbe (Laube), John and Mary Brower (Brauer), Georg Koth, Thomas Holeman (Hollmann or Hoelemann), Robert Ackerman, etc.

The oldest volume of the county-records, kept at Henrico Courthouse at Richmond, Va., referring to inheritances, criminal investigations, etc., mentions as prosecutors, defendants and witnesses among many names that may just as well be English as German, the following Germans:

> 1677—William Hand, Th. Gregory, John Bowman (Baumann.)
>
> 1678—Margarete Horner.
>
> 1679—John Gunter (Guenther), Katherine Knibbe, Georg Kranz and Thos. Risboc, — the last two in German letters.

1680—Thom. Brockhouse (Brockhaus), Georg Archer, John Harras and W. T. Eller, — the last three in partial German writing.

1681—J. Tanner, Edm. Bollcher, Rob. Bolling, Th. Grouse (Krause), and in German writing: John Feil.

1682-86—Doll, Rich. Starke, Mary Skirme, Henry Shurmann (that is: Schuermann, — in later entries the same man signs: Sherman), — Thos. Ruck, Joshua Stap (probably Stapf), and in German letters: Will. Blachman.

Taking in consideration the small number of white settlers, these German names in the registers and records of a single county, which was at the time still predominantly inhabited by Indians, are proof that the German immigration was numerally worthy of notice.

The limits of the counties of Norfolk and Princess Ann originally from 1637 to 1691 formed "Lower Norfolk County." Edward W. James mentions in his "Antiquary" among the earliest landowners the following names of German sound: Samuel Boush, John Weblin, Thos. Wishart, Capt. James Kempe, Wm. Wishart, Thos. and Wm. Brock, Robert Waller, Jeremiah and Matthew Forman, L. Miller, Abrah. Mesler, Robert Fry (schoolmaster of Norfolk Borough), Wm. Plume (member of the Common Council, Norfolk Borough), John Boush (Mayor of Norfolk Borough 1791), Daniel Bedinger (member of a Court of Aldermen), and others.

The population was, as has been mentioned, heavily oppressed during the government of Sir Berkeley, and dissatisfaction was spreading. The English high-church by its intolerance greatly furthered the rebellious spirit. The peaceable Quakers were especially made to suffer. However, the immediate cause of the outbreak of the revolution was the renewed depredations of the Indians in revenge for the treacherous murder of some of their chiefs.

Alarmed and disgusted by the inefficient measures for defence taken by governor Berkeley, the indignant settlers rose in opposition in 1676. They asked permission to arm and defend themselves and to appoint Nathaniel Bacon, a patriotic young lawyer, their leader. This the governor, fearing to put arms in the hands of the discontented men, and jealous of

Bacon's popularity, refused; while the savages continued to commit many outrages on the planters. Bacon now put himself at the head of his followers, defeated the Indians and then turned round against the governor, who had declared him a traitor. He drove Sir Berkeley and his adherents from Jamestown and the town was partly destroyed. Bacon died suddenly, and there was not a second man brave and worthy enough to take his place. Berkeley recovered his power and wreaked vengeance on the patriots by confiscations and executions until the thoughtless and profligate King Charles II declared: "The old fool has taken away more lives in that naked country, than I for the murder of my father!" — However, Bacon's rebellion, as this revolution is called, foreshadowed the great war of Independence and the end of English tyranny. It is a remarkable coincidence, that Drummond, one of the supporters of Bacon, was beheaded on the same spot where a hundred years later Lord Cornwallis surrendered to the superior tactics and strategy of George Washington and his German general von Steuben, assisted by the French allied army.

In 1677 governor Berkeley was discharged from office and for the space of 31 years the king granted the colony to Lords Culpepper and Arlington. The first named was appointed governor for life. He came over in 1680, but trying only to get as much money as possible out of his province, another rebellion was threatening, when the king, for fear of its results, revoked the grant and recalled Culpepper. His successor, Lord Howard, was little better, he also deemed Virginia his "milk cow," and it is really surprising that in spite of all the ill-treatment and mismanagement the colony prospered. In the year 1671 there were 40,000 white inhabitants in Virginia, and at the end of the seventeenth century the population nearly reached 100,000.

3. THE FIRST GERMANS IN NEW YORK

By

John O. Evjen

This chapter is a facsimile of material which originally appeared in John O. Evjen's *Scandinavian Immigrants in New York, 1630-1674*, Minneapolis: Holter, 1916.

In the Preface to our work it is shown that, judging by Prof. Flom's scholarly "A History of Norwegian Immigration" and by Mr. Holand's more popular "De norske Settlementers Historie," the immigration of Scandinavians to New York in the seventeenth century must have been practically (and professionally) a *terra incognita* as late as 1909, when these authors published their works.

Much the same may be said in regard to the German immigration to New York during the Dutch rule, if we judge by Prof. Albert Bernhardt Faust's (Cornell University) "The German Element in the United States," published in the same year. This standard-work, submitted in a contest to the Germanic Department of the University of Chicago, obtained for the author the first prize, $3000, given by Mrs. Catherine Seipp, of Chicago. Excellent as Prof. Faust's work is, it makes only two statements that might permit of a conclusion as to the numerical strength of the Germans in New Netherland.

The first is this:

"There were Germans in the Dutch settlement of New Netherland, and among them two who were second to none in moulding the destinies of the colony. The one was the first governor of New Netherland, Peter Minuit, and the other the first governor of New York to represent the popular party, Jacob Leisler."

The second reads:

"Dwelling with the Dutch settlers of New Amsterdam, there was undoubtedly quite a sprinkling of Germans. A good example is that of Dr. Hans Kierstede, who came from Magdeburg in 1638 with Director Kieft. He was the first practising physician and surgeon in that colony. He married Sarah Roelofse, daughter of Roeloff and Anneke Janse, the owner of the Annetje Jans farm on Manhattan Island."

The latter statement is somewhat hypothetical. The former is rather indefinite. They offer nothing tangible for answering the question, How great was this sprinkling? Professor Faust makes mention of no other Germans in New Netherland than Minuit, Kierstede, Augustin Herman, and Leisler. Though his treatment of Minuit is as elucidating as his description of the activities of Leisler is sympathetic, he fails to call attention to German leaders like Schrick, Ebbing, Van Beeck, Burger Joris, and Nicholaes De Meyer the burgomaster of New York city in 1676.

This criticism does not aim to detract anything from the value of Prof. Faust's splendid contribution to the history of the German element in our country. Its object is merely to indicate that the German immigrants in New York 1630—1674 have received no more attention than the Scandinavian.

As the background for a treatment of these German immigrants would be much the same as what our volume outlines in treating the immigrants from the Scandinavian countries, we venture in the present Appendix to register the names, with more or less pertinent data, of some 180 immigrants from various cities and districts of Germany, including a few from Switzerland and Austria. The list does not claim to be exhaustive. A more extended examination of the sources will increase the number of names, and, of course, add to the data, which I have collected, but of which I here present only a part.

Prof. Faust states a fact when he says that October 6, 1683, is "the date celebrated by all Germans in America as the beginning of their history in the United States." But we believe that the history of the Germans in the leading state of the United States begins (like that of the Scandinavians) more than a half century earlier.

Long before 1683, scores of places in Germany were represented in New Netherland and registered in the records of the Empire State.

It is as if a part of the history of the Middle Ages and the era of the Reformation passes in review before us when the records present names as these: *Aachen, Stade, Fulda, Wrede,*

Wesel, Eisleben, Mansfeld, Magdeburg, Worms, Jena, Augsburg,
Nürnberg, Hesse, Zürichsee, Bern, Mülhausen, Münster, Tübingen,
They are suggestive of the coronation of emperors, of monastic-
ism; of a forerunner of the Reformation; of the history of Luther
and diets; of a Philip of Hesse; of Zwingli; of the Peasants' War
and the Anabaptists; of the theological efforts of Andrea to re-
store peace among contending theologians.

And what a variety of associations are connected with names
like *Bremen, Hamburg, Lübeck, Cologne, Frankfurt am Main,*
Berlin, Königsberg, Wolfenbüttel, Erlangen, Giessen, Berg, Bonn,
Bocholt, Borken, Brunswick, Emden, Ems, Elberfeld, Elsfleth,
Falkenburg, Gemen, Herborn, Hirschberg, Hammelwarden, Jever,
Johannisberg, Lauffen, Lemgo, Lippstad, Kremmen, Mannheim,
Osnabrück, Rodenkirchen, Soest, Struckhausen, Xanten; and
Baden, Berg-Cassel, Cleves, East Friesland, Jülich, Oldenburg,
Waldeck, Westphalia. Even *Transylvania* and *Prague* are repre-
sented, and the name "Das 'Kayserreych'" is not failing.

But enough. These places together with the one hundred and
eighty men and women who represented them in New Netherland
before the close of the Dutch Dominion on American soil are sufficient to merit at least the brief treatment that is accorded them
in the present Appendix, which endeavors only to call attention to
the fact that the Germans, no less than the Scandinavians, were
by no means a *quantité négligeable* in the history of New York,
1630—1674.

Like the Dutch, the Germans and Scandinavians are Teutons.
They have the same civilization. And yet, so far as New York is
concerned, the German and Scandinavian immigrant in the seventeenth century had more in common with each other than with
the Dutch:

First, the majority of the German pioneers had the same
creed as the Scandinavian: They were Lutherans.

Secondly, in number they were inferior to the Dutch, who
had some reason for priding themselves on being natives from
what was then the most flourishing state in Europe. Moreover,
these sons of Germany, Sweden, Denmark, Norway were not so
apt as the Dutch immigrants to overlook difficulties and expect
immediate rewards.

What Mr. J. K. Riker says of the pioneers of Harlem also holds true, it would seem, of the entire population of New Netherland: "Though the Dutch and French elements were dominant in giving tone to the community, the Scandinavians and Germans, few in number . . . were second to none for sterling common sense, while foremost to bear danger and hardship, to wield the axe whose ring first startled the slumbering forest, or to turn the first furrow in the virgin soil."

Mr. Riker's contention is supported by the court records. They reveal that the German and Scandinavian element on the whole showed a greater respect for law and order than the more adventurous elements from Dutch- and French-speaking Netherlands of Europe.

As to the creedal factor, the Scandinavians were Lutherans "by birth" so to speak. Their native states recognized no other creed than the Lutheran. As this creed was not tolerated by the Governor and Council of New Netherland, who were bent on keeping the Reformed creed (especially the canons of the Synod of Dort) the state religion of New Netherland, — the Scandinavians , in their efforts to get religious liberty, received allies in the Lutheran immigrants from Germany. The majority of these German pioneers were Lutherans of the seventeenth century type; though not a few of them, coming from the western part of Germany, were Reformed or Roman Catholic.

Settled in New York, a number of these Lutherans, both German and Scandinavian, joined the Reformed church. They intermarried among the Reformed. But the large majority adhered to the "faith of their fathers," even if this adherence at times savored of "zeal without knowledge." This majority had a common enemy in the politico-ecclesiastical measures of the Governor and Council, and found little or no sympathy with the Dutch colonists, who in ecclesiastical matters were of the same cloth as Stuyvesant. In fact, the *Dutch* Lutherans in early New York were hardly in evidence. The story that the oldest Lutheran church in New Netherland was Dutch, lies hard by the realm of myths.

The first Lutheran church in New Netherland was cosmopolitan;* perhaps better, essentially German-Scandinavian — with

---

* I have made this statement before: in Ruoff's "Volume Library," p. 404; "Realencyclopädie fuer protestantische Theologie und Kirche" v. XXIV, 538 (Leipzig, 1913), edited by Albert Hauck.

emphasis on German. It is significant that the petition of the Lutherans in New Amsterdam, 1657, requesting that Rev. Goetwater be permitted to remain in New Amsterdam, appears to have been signed by *sixteen* Germans, *five* Scandinavians and *three* Hollanders. (pp. 37 fl.)

It is also significant that the Reformed preachers in New Amsterdam expressly mention *Paul Schrick*, from Nürnberg, as the leader among the Lutherans (p. 88); *Pieter Jansen* as a "northerner," "stupid" enough to take sides with the Lutherans in discussing baptism (p. 87); the Norwegian, *Laurence Noorman*, as a Lutheran sponsor and as the host who for a winter concealed the Lutheran minister on his farm (p. 39) when the government had ordered him to go into exile; and *Magdelene Kallier* (-Waele), a Scandinavian woman, as a godparent. These preachers do not complain, however, of Dutch Lutherans. And the records tell nothing about squabbles between Dutch Reformed preachers and *Dutch* Lutheran laymen, though they do not fail to set forth the dispute, in 1680, between Rev. Gideon Schaets, Dutch Reformed minister of Albany, and Meyndert Fredricksen, a *German* Lutheran.

Does not this indicate that the Dutch Lutherans, in proportion to the German and Scandinavian, were too few in number or too much wanting in aggressiveness?

And, does not the presence of a man like Jan Goetwater as the first Lutheran minister in New Amsterdam indicate the preponderance of the German element in the church he was to serve? The Reformed preachers at times called him "Goetwater," though "Gutwasser" was the form he used in signing his name. Was "Goetwater" his real name? If so, "Gutwasser" is a Germanization of it, showing that strong German influences likely were at work in the circle he was sent over to serve. It is more probable, however, that "Gutwasser" is the original; and that the bearer of this name was a German, who was at home in the Dutch language as well as in his native tongue. The Consistory of Amsterdam presumably acted according to the desire of Paulus Schrick and his countrymen when they sent over to New Netherland a preacher, who probably was of German extraction, but could preach in Dutch.

As has been indicated in various places in our book, the Lutherans in New Netherland were not allowed the exercise of public worship according to the dictates of their conscience or in harmony with their creed. It was the policy of the new government whose subjects they were to make and keep the Reformed "religion" the religion of the entire province.

This policy was not a new one. In 1638 the government proclaimed that "every man shall be free to live up to his own conscience in peace and decorum; provided he avoid frequenting any forbidden assemblies or conventicles, much less collect or get any such." This proclamation was confirmed, in reality explained, in the West India Company's New Charter of Patroonship, 1640, which specified that "no other religion shall be publicly admitted to New Netherland except the Reformed, as it is at present preached and practiced by the public authority in the United Netherlands."

The Council waived this, however, so far as the English were concerned. It proclaimed in 1641 that the "English shall have free exercise of their religion." It also decreed when New Sweden was conquered, 1655, that the Swedes living there should be permitted to adhere to the Augsburg Confession and to have their own minister. But these concessions were dictated by policy, and not by principle.

The English Independents were as little recognized as were the Lutherans. The "fate" of the Independents was also the "fate" of the Lutherans, Mennonites, Quakers and Catholics. Stuyvesant and his predecessors in office were not able to comprehend the spirit of liberty, which found such energetic spokesmen as Gustavus Adolphus and Oliver Cromwell.

And therefore, even as late as February, 1656, the Director-General and Council regarded it as their duty to decree the following:

"The Director General and Council have credibly been informed, that not only conventicles and meetings are held here and there in this Province, but that also unqualified persons presume in such meetings to act as teachers in interpreting and expounding God's holy Word without ecclesiastical or temporal authority. This is contrary to the general political and ecclesiastical rules of our Fatherland and besides such gatherings lead to troubles, heresies and schisms. Therefore to prevent this the Director General and Council strictly forbid all such public or private conventicles and meetings, except the usual and authorized ones, where God's reformed ordained Word is preached and taught in a meeting for the reformed divine service conform to the Synod of Dort and followed here as well as in the Fatherland and other reformed churches of Europe, under a fine of 100 pounds of Flemish to be paid by all, who in such public or private meetings, except the usual authorized gatherings, on Sunday or other days presume to exercise without due qualification the duties of a preacher, reader or precentor and each man or woman, married or unmarried, who are found at such a meeting, shall pay a fine of 25 pounds Flemish [= $60.00]. The Director General and Council do not however hereby intend to force the consciences, to the prejudice of formerly given patents, or to forbid the preaching of God's holy Word, the family prayers and divine service in the family, but only all public and private conventicles and gatherings, be they in public or private houses, except the already mentioned usual and authorized reformed divine service. In order that this order may be better observed and nobody plead ignorance thereof the Director General and Council direct and charge their Fiscal and the inferior Magistrates and Schouts, to publish it everywhere in this Province and prosecute the transgressors, whereas we have so decreed it for the honor of God, the advancement of the Reformed service and the quiet, unity and welfare of the country in general.

"Thus done etc., February 1, 1656."

The Directors in United Netherlands were not altogether pleased with this placard, and still less with Stuyvesant's enforcing of it. For, according to a letter of the Directors, in June of the same year, Stuyvesant actually committed some Lutherans to prison. It reads:

"We would have been better pleased, if you had not published the placard against the Lutherans, a copy of which you sent us, and committed them to prison, for it has always been our intention, to treat them quietly and leniently. Hereafter you will therefore not publish such or similar placards without our knowledge, but you must pass it over quietly and let them have free religious exercises in their houses."

The sources accessible to us do not give the names of these prisoners or help us to establish the accuracy of the statement in regard to any imprisoning of Lutherans. Perhaps the Directors in United Netherlands were laboring under some misapprehension. The probability, however, is that Stuyvesant did what the letter claimed he did. It suffices to mention his subsequent treatment of Rev. Goetwater.

The Lutherans in New Amsterdam, while obediently acting upon the prohibitive order of February, 1656, received word from their friends in United Netherlands (who had interceded for them there with the Directors of the West India Company) that the Directors "in a full meeting" resolved that the doctrines of the Unaltered Augsburg Confession should be tolerated in the West Indies and New Netherland "under their jurisdiction, in the same manner as in the Fatherland, under its excellent government."

The Lutherans in New Netherland informed Stuyvesant and the Council in regard to this, October 24, 1656, praying "that henceforth we may not be hindered in our services. These with Gods blessing we intend to celebrate, with prayer, reading and singing, until, as we hope and expect, a qualified person shall come next spring from the Fatherland to be our minister and teacher, and remain here as such."

But the Council at New Amsterdam would make no concession, and simply reiterated that no one should be prevented from having family worship. Public worship was to remain under the same restriction as before.

Meanwhile Rev. Jan Goetwater arrived in the summer of 1657. But the Reformed pastors sent in to the Burgomasters and Schepens their objections against his taking up any pastoral work among the Lutherans in New Netherlands. Among the objections were these:

If the Lutherans should have public worship, the result would be "great contention and discord" not only among the inhabitants and citizens in general, but also in families, "of which we have had proofs and complaints during the past year. For example, some husbands have forced their wives to leave their own church, and attend their conventicles." Secondly, the numbers of hearers in the Reformed church would be "perceptibly diminished. Many of that persuasion [Lutheran] have continued attentive hearers among us, and several have united themselves with our church.

These would separate themselves from us." Thirdly, "the treasury of our deacons [the poor fund] would be considerably diminished. and become unable to sustain the burdens it has hitherto borne," as "there is no other means provided for the support of the poor, save what is collected in the church." Fourthly, "if the Lutherans should be indulged in the exercise of their (public) worship, the Papists, Mennonites and others would soon make a similar claim. Thus we would soon become a Babel of confusion, instead of remaining a united and peaceful people. Indeed it would prove a plan of Satan to smother this infant rising congregation, almost in its birth, or at least to obstruct the march of truth in its progress."

The Burgomasters and Schepens were pleased with these arguments, and adopted measures accordingly. They summoned Rev. Goetwater. They charged him not to hold any public or private religious exercises in New Amsterdam, and informed the Director General and Council of what their views were and what they had done. This latter body and Stuyvesant ratified their action, and requested them strictly to enforce the placard of February, 1656. Goetwater got orders to leave the country.

The Reformed ministers now sent a report, Aug. 5, 1657, to the Classis of Amsterdam, stating that they could not have believed that the Directors in United Netherlands should have permitted the Lutherans to have public worship. But they were disillusionized when Rev. Goetwater arrived, as they wrote, "to the great joy of the Lutherans, but to the special displeasure and uneasiness of the congregation in this place; yea, even the whole country, including the English, were displeased." They urged that Goetwater, "the snake in our bosom", be sent back to Holland.

It was now that the Lutherans sent in their well known petition of Oct. 10, 1657, so often referred to in this volume, and given in full on page 37 ff. The Reformed ministers later claimed that this petition was "signed by the least respectable" of the Lutherans, and that "the most influential among them were unwilling to trouble themselves with it."

Their petition of October 10, followed by a letter from Rev. Goetwater to the Director General and Council, proved to be in vain. Goetwater was again commanded to leave the country.

But he was in no hurry to depart.

He remained during the winter of 1657—58 at the farm of a Norwegian. (See p. 39.) His opponents, the Reformed minister wrote that Goetwater, instead of returning to Holland "went out of the city and concealed himself with a Lutheran farmer during the whole winter," where the congregation "supported him at the rate of six guilders ($2.40) per week. On the fourth of August last, when we celebrated the Lord's Supper, they made a collection among themselves for him. The Fiscal was again directed to arrest him, and compel him to leave by one of the earliest ships. In the meantime the Lutherans came and represented to the Director-General that their preacher was sick at the farmer's, and besought the privilege of bringing him within the place for treatment. This was granted them. The Fiscal was at the same time empowered to watch over him, and when well again to send him to Holland. Whether on his recovery, he will return or conceal himself again, time must show."

The Council not long thereafter, on November 11, 1658. passed a resolution, that Goetwater "remain in New Amsterdam until otherwise directed." He did not preach, however.

Stuyvesant did all in his power to make Lutheran preaching in New Netherland an utter impossibility. In 1662 he again published a proclamation against the preaching of any other than the Reformed doctrine "either in houses, barns, ships or yachts, in the woods and fields."

Not before the English conquered New Netherland, in 1664. did the Lutherans in this colony get a "charter," granting them the right of free and public exercise of divine worship according to their conscience; provided they would "not abuse this liberty to the disturbance of others . . ."

This "charter" was far from implying complete parity. It did not mean autonomy. And when the Dutch, in 1675, reconquered their territory, the Lutherans were legally in the same position as before, petitioning anew for permission to exercise public worship. But the Dutch government proved more liberal now than before. It permitted the free exercise of worship to the Lutherans (September, 1673), but forbade, in March, 1674, Jacobus Fabritius. Lutheran pastor from Grosglogan in Silesia. to act as clergyman for a year, because he had solemnized a marriage, without having been lawfully authorized to act as clergyman. This attitude to a clergyman that in 1669 had received permission from Governor Lovelace to become pastor of the Lutherans in New York and Albany, shows that the Dutch government was in continuity with itself, though it was trying to follow a more lenient policy than before. Fabritius, who preached in Dutch, but seems to have been a Pole, had already at the outset proved himself a troublesome clergyman, quarreling with his parishioners and the state authorities: he had domestic troubles, and now and then got drunk. He was obliged to resign in 1670, and became the pastor of the Swedes on the Delaware. But his weakness is no excuse for the sentence imposed upon him by the restored Dutch rule under Colve.

After the restoration of the English rule, in 1674, the Lutherans enjoyed their rights as before. Fabritius, however, fared no better. The Swedish and Finnish Lutherans at Cranehook remonstrated against him in August, 1675, because they could not understand his language. In September, in the same year, the English government again suspended him "from exercising his function as a minister, or preaching any more within this government either in public or private." The reason for this suspension was his "irregular life and conversation."

The treatment of Rev. Goetwater by the Dutch Government, the sad experiences with his successor who was morally unfit for his position may have discouraged the Lutherans, and caused that a number of them joined the Reformed church. Meanwhile the differences between the Reformed and Lutherans were gradually disappearing in the consciousness of the common people, though the problem of election caused ill feeling among members of the respective denominations as late as 1680.

Later, when James II. ascended the throne of England, the fear that Catholicism would become a power in the colonies drew the contending Protestants in New Netherland closer together. And the spirit of Protestantism, whether originally imbibed from the Lutheran "doctrine" or from the Reformed "religion" or both, was at the close of the century so strong that the attempt to make even the Episcopal church the state church of New York proved abortive.

This is not the place to indulge in denominational polemics. But the fact that Germans and Scandinavians played an important role in the life of our present metropolis is a factor that must be reckoned with in considering the religious developments in early New York.

As for the political influence, it suffices to point to a Dane like Captain Kuyter, to Germans like Mayor Nicholas de Meyer and Governor Jacob Leisler.

We can not here discuss the social, economic, and industrial assets of the early German immigrants. The list * of names immediately following may throw a little light on these and kindred questions. For us it is sufficient to point out the Germans in polyglot New Netherland, and to assist in giving an impulse to the study of the German element in the United States prior to 1683; yes, prior to 1674, when the Dutch rule, excellent as it was in many ways, gave way to the rule that was to obtain for a whole century but ended in the American Revolution.

LIST OF GERMAN IMMIGRANTS IN NEW YORK
1630—1674.

Jan Adamsen (Metselaer-Messler) was born at *Worms,* Germany, 1626, died 1696. His name appears in the court records of New Amsterdam in 1656. In 1665 he lived in Marketfield Alley. In 1669 he was one of the curators of the estate of Hage Bruynsen, a Swede (p. 306). His sons, Sebastian, Dirck, Abraham, Isaac were born in 1658, 1661, 1662, 1678 respectively. Of these, Abraham married, 1694, Harmetje Gerrits.

Barent Andriessen, from *Wrede* in Westphalia, married, in 1654, Elken Jans "van Voorden, int Graefschap Zutphen." They lived in New Amsterdam. Two years later, Andriessen was dead, the widow having married Thomas Franszen, of Boston.

Hans Albertsen, from *Brunswick,* got land in September, 1656, near Roelof Jansen de Haes, a Norwegian, in New Amsterdam. In 1658 he is mentioned in the court records, as a witness in a lawsuit.

---

* Immigrants from Schleswig and Holstein have been treated in Part II.

Harmon Arentsen was in New Amsterdam in 1644 (or earlier), when he was thirty-eight years old. He was from *Bremen.*

*

Jan Barentszen, of *Lübeck,* married in New Amsterdam, 1685, Maryken Jillis, widow of Robert Rotges. In 1694 he married Marritie Webbers.

Meyndert Barentszen, from *Jever,* in *Oldenburg* married in New Amsterdam, June 6, 1659, Anneke Cornelis. In October, 1657, he signed the petition of the Lutherans, requesting that Rev. Goetwater be retained as a Lutheran pastor in New Amsterdam. He was a cooper, and had several hired men. In 1665 he lived in Smith Street. He got the small burgher's right in New Amsterdam, 1657. He had children.

Paulus van der Beeck, from *Bremen,* married, 1644, in New Amsterdam, Maria Thomas, widow of Willem de Cuper. In 1657 he was farmer of weigh scales; in 1660 farmer of burgher excise of wine and beer. In his official capacity he was often in court, prosecuting. He owned several lots in New Amsterdam. In 1662 he let a contract for a house "40 ft. × 20 ft. × 6 ft." He was one of the leading citizens in New Amsterdam.

Cornelis Beckman, from Stift *Bremen,* married, in 1665, in New Amsterdam, Marritje Cornelis, widow of Hans Ketel, or Hans Christiaenszen. She was from Flensburg (p. 185).

Jochem Beeckman was in New Amsterdam in 1639 or before. He was a cobbler by trade. He had a quick hand and a ready tongue wherewith to defend himself, what brought him several times into court. His wife was a faithful ally in matters of self-defense. He was in all probability a German, as he is seen to have associated much with Germans, being frequently called in as sponsor in German families. In October, 1657, he signed the petition of the Lutherans that they might retain Rev. Goetwater as Lutheran pastor in New Amsterdam. He had a house and lot on the east side of Heere Graft, "to the North of Pine St., to the East the house and lot of Jacobus Baker, West the said Gracht." He had children.

Christina Bleyers, from "Stoltenon" in *Lüneburg,* was married, Jan. 17, 1659, in New Amsterdam, to Pieter Hendricksen Christians, from Denmark (p. 186).

Adam Brouwer Berkhoven immigrated to New Netherland from *Cologne,* in 1642. He married Mag(reta) Jacobs Verdon. In 1677—80 he and his wife were members of the Dutch Reformed Church at Brooklyn.

Matys Blanjan (Blanchan), from *Mannheim,* is mentioned in the records of New Amsterdam in 1662, when reference is also made to his son-in-law. Matys Blanjan jr. married in Kingston, N. Y., 1679. As there were in New Amsterdam several Frenchmen from Mannheim, Matys may have been one of them. He was a Protestant.

Jan Bosch, from *Westphalia,* arrived at New Amsterdam, by the ship "de Vos," which sailed from Texel, August 31, 1662. When the English Governor, in 1665, desired to billet off soldiers, Bosch claimed he could not receive soldiers, as "he has no bed" for them.

He is mentioned in the court records as late as 1674. He was dead before May, 1679, when his widow, Rachel Vermelje, married Dirck Wesselsen, from Arnhem.

Adam Bremen, from *Aachen,* sailed for New Amsterdam Dec. 23, 1657, by "de Jan Baptiste." His wife, Elsie Barents, and a servant girl followed in 1663, by "de Bonte Koe." He was dead before 1670, when his widow married Marius de Vos.

Aeltie Van Bremen is mentioned, in 1668, in the records of New Netherland. She is probably the woman who was married, 1643, at New Amsterdam, to *Pieter Collet,* from *Königsberg.*

Michiel Bronval is listed among the passengers, who were to sail for New Netherland, by "de Bonte Koe," April 15, 1660. He was from *Berg-Cassel,* and probably sailed as a soldier.

Albert Buer, from *Jülich,* sailed for New Amsterdam, April 8, 1662, by the ship "de Hoop."

Johannes Burger, from Gemen (*Münster*) is mentioned in the records of New Amsterdam in 1663. In 1691 he married Helena Turck.

*

Claes van Campen, of *Oldenburg,* is designated as a farmer boy in the records of New Netherland, 1660.

Matthys Capito, surnamed Boon, Bon, Bontze, was probably from *Bonn,* Germany. In August, 1650, in New Amsterdam, he married Elsje Pieters, from *Hamburg,* widow of Hans Webber. Capito signed, in October, 1657, the petition of the Lutherans in New Amsterdam, requesting that Rev. Goetwater be allowed to remain as their pastor. In 1659 Capito was commissary at South River. After about the year 1660 he was secretary of the village of Esopus, mustermaster, secretary of the council of war (Indian wars were waged). He was schout of Wiltwyck, Dec. 1663— April, 1664. The name "Capito" is a Latinization of "Köpfel." Capito's wife was killed and burned in the Indian war at Esopus, 1663. He died about 1667. His name often occurs in the records of New Netherland. He figured frequently in the courts. He had at least one child: Hendrick, born in 1653. A letter of Capito, June 29, 1663, to Gov. Stuyvesant and the Council of New Netherland, speaks of his poverty after he had lost all he had in the war. It reads:

"Gentlemen. Whereas I, your Hon. Worships' humble petitioner have also been brought to ruin during these late troubles in the village of Wiltwyck, caused by the savages, not having lost only my dear wife, who was killed by the barbarians and then burned with the house, to which they set fire, but in the same fire also all my moveable effects, that nothing else is left to me, but my honest name. Now, as I need during my further life, for covering my body and keeping clean, some linen and cloth, which at present cannot be obtained here, and which, even if it were to be had here, I cannot pay for, therefore I am compelled to turn to your Hon. Worships, in pity of my distressed circumstances and misery; (you) will please to assist me and provide me with low-priced clothing, to-wit, some cheap plain cloth for a suit of clothes and what is needed for it, two or three store-shirts or linen to make them, one or one and a half els of linen for handkerchiefs and nightcaps, a blanket and enough coarse linen for a straw tick and a pillow, two pairs of Icelandish socks and a pair of shoes—and charge these goods according to their prices to my account. I promise to make it good to your Hon. Worships as soon as I can, and as with God's blessing I shall have again prospered somewhat. Not doubting that I expect to receive them by the first opportunity, because my needy circumstances require them, closing with greetings, I commend your Honr. Worships to the Almighty's protection, wishing and praying sincerely, that the good God will save your Honbl. Worships and us all from all such and similar misfortune and troubles while I remain Mateus Capito."

Gabriel Carbosie (Carpesy), born in *Lauffen,* near Mannheim, married, in New Amsterdam, 1657, Teuntje Straelsman. He later married Briete Olofs, a widow, from Sweden (p. 340).

Wolfgang Carstensen, soldier, from *Wolfenbüttel,* married July 3, 1660, in New Amsterdam, Elsje Jans Bresteede, widow of Hendrick Jansen.

Jan Christiaen (De Jon Christiaen), from *Germany,* was in New Netherland in April 1660.

Dirck Claeszen, from *Bremen,* married, in November, 1650, in New Amsterdam, Aechtje Jacobs (Van "Hertogenbusch"). He seems to have been a potter.

Valentine Claesen, from *"Saxenlant,* in Transylvania," married, April, 1662, in New Amsterdam, Maritje Beest, from "Cuylenborg." In 1673 he was Schepen of Fordham village. As Riker says, the Valentines of our country are not descendants of Benjamin Valentine, a French dragoon in French military service in Canada, but from Valentine Claesen.

Jan Van Cleef (Cleves) was in New Amsterdam as early as 1653, when he was twenty-five years of age. In company with Titus Cyre he bought a horsemill belonging to Jacob van Couwenhoven. He later became the sole owner of it, but soon sold it, what brought on considerable litigation in the court.

Ulderick Cleen, [Uldrich Klein], from *Hesse,* married, in July, 1641, in New Amsterdam, Afje Pieters, of Amsterdam. They had at least one child, baptized in 1642.

Cornelis Jansen Clopper, from *Kloppenborg,* petitioned, in 1655, the council of New Amsterdam for permission to tap. It appears that he had just returned from Brazil to New Amsterdam, where he had resided before he went to South America. He had been "driven away" from Brazil. He was a smith, and had hired workmen. In 1660 he acquired a parcel of ground in Smith's Valley. He served on the jury in 1667.

Johannes Clute came to Beverwyck about 1656 from *Nürnberg.* He was commonly called captain and was held in esteem by the Mohawks. He was a trader and large land-holder in Loonenburg, Niskayuna, and Albany. His name was sometimes spelled

Cloete. There were many in early New York who had the name Clute. Johannes died about 1684.

Hans or *Jans Coenratse* was from *Nürnberg.* He is mentioned in the records of New Netherland in 1660.

Hendrick Coenratse, from *Bonn,* was in New Netherland in 1660.

Pieter Collet, from *Königsberg* "in Pruysen," married, in August, 1643, in New Amsterdam, Aeltje Jans, from *Bremen,* widow of John Cornelisen, of Rotterdam. He signed the well-known resolution adopted by the Commonalty of Manhattans in October, 1643. He had a child baptized in December, 1644.

Jan Cornelissen de Ryck was probably a German. He married in May, 1658, in New Amsterdam, Marritje Gerrits. They had children. The Jan Cornelissen who, in October, 1657, signed the petition of the Lutherans, in New Amsterdam, to retain Rev. Goetwater as pastor is possibly Jan Cornelissen de Ryck. In 1671 Cornelissen was overseer of Roads.

Hendrick Corneliszen Van Valckenburg was, judging by the name, from *Falkenburg* in Germany, not far from Jülich. In May, 1650, he married, in New Amsterdam, Marie Bowens, from London. He seems to have been a rope maker.

Lambert van Valckenburch was in New Amsterdam as early as 1644, and received a patent of land there, March 16, 1647. He removed to Fort Orange. See Plate facing p. 62.

Jan Coster [Köster], of *Aachen,* bought a lot in Beverwyck in March, 1661. In 1669 he was called Jan van Aecken.

Barent Court [Coerten] "van Rhenen" in "Stift *Münster"* married in December, 1664, in New Amsterdam, Anna Jans, widow of Andries Spiering. He joined the Dutch Reformed Church in 1666. In 1686 his wife was Christina Wessells. They lived on High Street. His property in this street was, in 1674, valued at $8000.

Michael Croes, from *Danzig,* married in June, 1661, in New Amsterdam, Jannetje Theunis.

Coenraet Croos, from *Switzerland,* was among the soldiers to sail, April 15, 1660, by "de Bonte Koe," for New Netherland.

*

Hans Diederick, of *Isleven* [Eisleben] married, in New Amsterdam, 1664, Grietje Warnaerts, widow of Adriaen Hendr. Zips. In 1673 he was elected Lieutenant at the nomination of the town of Bergen, N. J. In 1684 he appears as a witness in a lawsuit.

Carsten Dircksen, from *Bremen,* a shoemaker by trade, got the small burgher's right in New Amsterdam, in 1657.

Jan Dircksen, from *Bremen,* was in New Amsterdam as early as 1639. In 1643 was skipper of a vessel, receiving orders from Kiliaen van Rensselaer. His wife was Tryntie Anders. They belonged to the Dutch Reformed church in New Amsterdam, and had a child baptized in February, 1644. In 1665 it appears that he had a scow, on which he employed hired men and took passengers. Dircksen was a "tar of the old sort," who loved strong drink and took pleasure in striking terror into his servants.

Lucas Dircksen, from *Berg,* Germany, was one of the signers of the Lutheran petition in October, 1657, in New Amsterdam. His wife was Annetje Cornelis. They had several children. Dircksen came to New Netherland in 1652 or before. In 1654 he was given a license to retail beer and wine. Up to that time he seems to have been employed as a soldier. His business brought him a number of times into court, — to collect an account or to be fined for tapping after the hours of closing. He seems to have resided for some time at South River, where he possessed a house.

Hans Dreper, or Draper (Drapier) was no doubt a Teuton. His signing the Lutheran petition in October, 1657, for retaining Rev. Goewater in New Amsterdam, and again a Lutheran petition at Albany, in 1673, seems to indicate that he was from Lutheran Scandinavia or Lutheran Germany. He was probably a German.

In 1654 he had a son baptized in New Amsterdam, and two years later a daughter. His wife was Marritie Pieters [also called Margritie Jans]. In October, 1656, Dreper requested by petition leave to tap beer and wines. The petition was granted. He had several lawsuits, prosecuting people for board and drink. He was often fined for using unbecoming language, and at one time even imprisoned for six weeks on bread and water. Also his wife was given to petty quarreling.

*

Hieronymus Ebbing, from *Hamburg,* married, in 1659, in New Amsterdam, Johanna de Laet, widow of John de Hulter. They had several children. Ebbing was for many years church warden of the Dutch Reformed church at New Amsterdam. In 1658 he supervised the paving of Brewer St. with cobblestones as an "ornament and for the use of the city." He was curator of the estate of the Dane Jochem Pietersen Kuyter. In 1658 he was made Great Burgher. He was elected schepen of the city in 1661, and was often re-elected. He had the title of Sieur. In 1665, living at Brewer Street, he was assessed fl. 4; only nine other citizens paying so high a tax. In 1670 he was juryman, and in 1673 was nominated burgomaster, but not elected. He often served as arbitrator in disputes.

Harmen Eduardsen (Eduwarsen) signed the petition of the Lutherans of New Amsterdam, 1657, to retain Rev. Goetwater. Eduardsen was probably a German. In 1662 we find him in Bergen, New Jersey, where he, in company with Laurens Andriessen Boskerk (p. 152) and others, subscribed money to defray the salary of a preacher. He owned some sixty-nine acres of land in Bergen. In 1674 he acquired land on Staten Island at the mouth of "Kill von Koll."

Elbert Elbertsen (Eldert Engelberts) from an island off the coast of East Friesland was at Midwout in 1654 or before. In March, 1656, he married, in New Amsterdam, Sarah Walker, of Boston. Their daughter Anna Maria was born in December of the same year at Maspeth Kills. Elbertsen was one of the "good men" in an arbitration suit in 1656, the other arbitrator being Domine Megapolensis. Riker's History of Harlem registers Elbertsen as a Swede. The spelling Engelberts would point to Swedish antecedents. It is probable though that, coming from East Friesland, he was German.

Lucas Eldertsen, from *Jever,* was in New Netherland as early as 1643, when his name occurs in the records of the colony of Rensselaerswyck. He was in New Amsterdam 1646. In 1649 he was given power of attorney by Jan Lawrensen Appel to collect money due at South River, when he is called "the worthy Luycas Eldertsen from Jeveren." In 1654 a son of Eldertsen and his wife, Annetje Jans, was baptized in New Amsterdam, and a daughter in 1656. In 1657 we find him as laborer at the weigh house. In the same year he signed the petition of the Lutherans requesting that Rev. Goetwater be retained as Lutheran pastor. In 1661 he was in Beverwyck. His widow married, in May, 1666, Laurens Jansen Van Wormer, a Hollander. Eldertsen seems to have been a person of quiet disposition, though he often appeared in court.

*

Hendrick Folckertsen, born in 1634, married Feb. 26, 1655, at New Amsterdam, Geertie Claes. He was from *Jever.* He acted as sponsor in 1654. In 1674 he is mentioned in the court records as intending to make a voyage to the West Indies. Folckertsen and his wife had at least one child.

Jurian Fradel, from *Moravia,* acquired sixty-nine acres of land at Long Island in September, 1644. A year later he, as the "husband of the widow of Hendrick Hendricksen," acquired some more land. He had a child baptized in New Amsterdam in 1653. Judging by the court records, he was a dealer in tobacco.

Arent Francken, a baker from *Jever,* arrived at New Amsterdam by the ship "de Trouw," which sailed February 12, 1659.

Carsten Frederickse, from *Jever,* a brother of Meyndert Fredericksen (see below), was a smith by trade (master smith). With his brother he had a smith shop in Albany; he owned also a lot on the north corner of Broadway and State Street. He was deacon of the Dutch Lutheran church, in the same city, 1680.

His wife was Tryntie Warners. They made a joint will July 1, 1689, which mentions their four children.

Meyndert Fredericksen, from *Jever,* married, in August, 1655, in New Amsterdam, Catharyn Burchart (Burger) ; and secondly, in 1663, Pietertje Teunise Van Vechten. They lived in the city of Albany. He was a smith and had together with his brother Karsten, a smith shop on the north corner of Broadway and Spanish (later Hudson) St. He was sometimes designated as "armorer to the fort." He was elder of the Dutch Lutheran church in Albany in 1680. In 1673 he signed a petition of the Lutherans, requesting in "their own and in the name of their congregation of the Augsburg Confession at Willemstadt (Albany) . . . in substance free exercise of their religious worship, without let or hindrance, to the end that they may live in peace with their fellow burghers. . . ." They had enjoyed religious liberty under the English rule, but the Dutch, on reconquering New Netherland in 1673, were less liberal. However, the local Dutch government ordered, on receipt of this petition: "The petitioners are granted and allowed their aforesaid request on condition of comporting themselves peaceably and quietly without giving any offence to the congregation of the Reformed Religion, which is the State Church (de hooft kercke)." In 1701 Meyndert signed another Lutheran petition addressed to King William III.

Meyndert and his wife were zealous defenders of Lutheranism, manifesting, however, a zeal which was deficient in knowledge, as will be seen from the minutes of the Extraordinary Court held at Albany in March, 1680. The problem of election occupied the lay Lutheran mind of our country even as early as the seventeenth century. It assumed such importance in the mind of Meyndert that he and his wife quarreled with the Reformed minister.

"The Court met at the request of Domine Gideon Schaets (Dutch Reformed minister at Albany) accompanied by the W. Consistory, who complains that Myndert Frederickse Smitt came to his house and told him, the Domine, never to presume to speak to any of his Children on religious matters; and that he, the Domine, went sneaking through all the houses like the Devil; adding, Our Domine (meaning Domine Bernardus, Minister of the Lutheran Congregation) does not do so.

"Domine Schaets further complains that Myndert Frederickse's wife grievously abused and calumniated him behind his back at Gabriel Thomson's house, as an old Rogue, Sneak, etc., and that if she had him by the pate, she should drag his grey hairs out of it; which the Domine offers to prove by witnesses.

"Whereupon Myndert Frederickse and wife are sent for to Court, and Domine Schaets' accusation is read to Myndert, who denies it all, declaring that he has not given the Domine an ill word.

"Pietertje, wife of Myndert Frederickse, denies having abused Domine Schaets as a rogue and sneak; but that the Domine hath abused her Religion as a Devilish Religion.

"Hend. Rooseboom sworn, says that he was at Gabriel Thomson's last Monday when Pietertje, Myndert Frederickse's wife, entered, and wishing to go away, was called back by Gabriel, and conversing on the subject of Domine Schaets and her daughter, she said,—What business hath Domine Schaets to question mine daughter? To this Gabriel said—Why should he not do so? The Domine does well to question people. Whereupon Pietertje said, Domine Schaets, the old Rogue and Sneak; had she been by she should have caught him by the grey pate—adding he ought to look to his daughter, the W. . . .e, and take care of her—To which Gabriel replied, Meutie, why say that and scold the Domine so? who answered him—You d . . . . dog! you protect your w . . . . . and knaves.

"Cornelis Teunise Swart, being sworn, says, he was also at Gabriel Thomson's last Tuesday, when Pietertje Myndert Frederickse's wife came in and enquired for her daughter, who not being there, she was going away, but Gabriel called her back and said—sit a while, Meutie; and being in conversation about Domine Schaets' wishing to question her daughter, she said she had, herself, a teacher to do so, that if she had the old rogue, she would take him by the grey pate, and further knoweth not."

"Mr. Sheriff Pretty requests their Worships that he may act herein, to institute his action, at a more convenient period.

"The W. Court postponed the matter to the next Court day to act on the merits. Meanwhile if parties can be reconciled, (through Respect for the Divine) they were particularly recommended to do so, saving Sheriff's action and costs."

On the next day the Court met again, when:

"Myndert Fredericksen and his wife appear before their Worships of the Court, requesting that they may be reconciled in love and friendship with Domine Schaets, as they have been with Gabriel. Whereupon their W. recommended him to call Domine Schaets, which being immediately done;

"Domine Schaets appearing before their Worships is asked—if he were willing to be reconciled with the aforesaid persons? who answers, Yes, on the condition that they both acknowledge him an honorable man, and that they know nought of him except what is honest and virtuous (always excepting the Dispute, out of which this Case arose, namely—Universal Grace—being no political question)*, also the Sheriff's claim.

"Whereupon Myndert aforesaid and his wife acknowledge the Domine in open Court to be an honest man,† and they know nought of him except all honor and virtue and are willing to bear all the costs hereof, also to settle with the Sheriff.

"N. B. It is settled by And. Teller and for six Beavers and six cans of wine!" (Ecclesiastical Records of the State og New York, I., p. 737f.)

In his will, 1704, proved May, 1706, Meyndert mentioned his "house and lot hard by the church in Cow St. (now Broadway), Albany, his garden behind the fort, and personal property, including a great silver tankard, a church book with silver clasps and chain, a silver tumbler, marked F . . . He had four children.

---

* This is explained by the following testimony in another case—"Hans Dreper further says that Gabriel's wife stated that Domine Schaets said at her house that whoever taught that Christ died alike for all men, taught a false and devilish Doctrine.

† The Domine's daughter was not without blame. Though unmarried she was the mother of a child by van Curler.

Cornelis Gerloffs, a tailor from *East Friesland*, came to New Amsterdam in 1661 by the ship "Gulden Arent," which sailed January 1, of that year. However, he had lived in New Amsterdam before, as the court records indicate.

Claes Gerritsen, son of Gerrit Lubbertsen, from *Wesel*, came to New Amsterdam by the ship "het Gekruijste Hart," sailing April 17, 1664. In 1671 he worked as a hired man.

Otto Grimm, from *Bremen*, married, in September, 1664, in New Amsterdam, Elsje Jans, widow of Elbert Jans. In the documents he is styled "captain at arms." In 1671 his wife, called Elsie Grimm, was sued by Jochem Beeckman. The records do not give any details as to this suit, only stating that, "Parties agreed." In 1674 Grimm's house in the present Broad St. was valued at $1,000.

Margaret Grootjen, from *Aachen*, married on June 11, 1660, in New Amsterdam, Barent Christoffelszen Cruydop, widower of Ursel Coenrats.

*

George Hanel, one of the signers of the petition of the Lutherans in New Amsterdam, 1657, requesting that Rev. Goetwater might be permitted to remain in the country as Lutheran minister, was probably a German. He is also later mentioned in the records of New Netherland, even as late as 1663. In the court records he is called Jurien Hanel. A "George Hans [Holmes]" signed the Resolution of the Commonalty of Manhattan, 1643. Is he George or Jurien Hanel?

Hendrick Hansen arrived in New Netherland in 1663, by "de Rooseboom," which sailed March 15, 1663. In the passenger's list it is said that he was "from *Germany*." Was he the mayor of Albany in 1698?

Jan Harberding [Harpendinck], from "Boeckholdt" [Bocholt] in Westphalia, married, in December, 1667, in New Amsterdam, Mayken Barents, from Harlem [New York?]. He was a shoemaker by occupation. In 1674 his property on the north side of the present Stone St., between William and Broad St., was valued at $3,000. He joined the Dutch Reformed church in April, 1664.

Johannes Hardenbroeck, from *Elberfeld,* arrived, with his wife, Urseltje Duytman, and four children, in New Netherland by the ship "de Trouw," which sailed January 20, 1664. The children were eight, six, five and three years old respectively. In 1665 he lived at the Prince Graft, in New Amsterdam. He became a prominent man in this city, often serving on the jury. An Abel Hardenberg (Obel Hardenbroeck), often referred to in the court records, and a well-to-do person, was possibly a relative of Johannes. The latter, it seems, was also ensign of the militia. He joined the Dutch Reformed church in 1686.

Melem Harloo, from the province of *"Middelsaxen,"* married in July, 1644, in New Amsterdam, Elsje Jans, widow of Jan Pietersen.

Frederick Harmenszen, from *Bremen,* was a member of the Dutch Reformed Church in New Amsterdam in 1649.

Hans Jacob Harting, from *Bern,* Switzerland, married in July, 1668, in New Amsterdam, Gertje Lambertsen Mol.

Claes Hayen, from *Bremen,* sailed for New Netherland in the ship "de Bonte Koe," April 15, 1660. He was an "Adelborst." He married Marritje Claes.

Cornelis Hendricksen, from *Ens* [Ems?], was probably a German. He came to New Netherland in "de Vergulde Bever," which sailed May 17, 1658.

Gerrit Hendricksenz, from *"Waerdenbroeck" in Cleves,* married in 1654, in New Amsterdam, Hermken Hermans, widow of Wilhelm Jansen. Gerrit acquired land in the vicinity of New Amsterdam as early as 1646. In 1663 he acquired land on the Schuykill. In 1658 he was farmer of excise in New Amsterdam, which office he continued to hold for several years. As such he often appeared in court to transact business. He was deceased in 1671.

Hendrick Hendricksen, from *Westphalia,* came to New Amsterdam by the ship "de Rooseboom," which sailed March 15, 1663. There were many Hendrick Hendricksens in New Amsterdam, including an Irishman. One was a drummer, another a tailor, a third a soldier, etc. To find the data for each particular person bearing this name in ancient New York, is a hopeless task.

Hendricks Hendricksen, from *Erlangen,* was in New Amsterdam in 1664 (or before), when he is mentioned as plaintiff in a court proceeding. In the same year his daughter Catharyntie was married to Jonas Ranzow, of Holstein (see p. 273). A Hendrick Hendricksen signed the Lutheran petition of 1657, requesting that Rev. Goetwater be permitted to stay in the country as Lutheran minister. Was it the one from Erlangen?

Huybert Hendricksen, from *Rodenkirchen* (near Cologne), married, January, 1656, in New Amsterdam, Marritje Hendricks Van Norden in East Friestland. They had several children. In 1663 he brought suit against Francis de Bruyn for tobacco. In 1665 he lived in Brewer St. He was still living in 1672. when he stood sponsor for a child belonging to John Otten.

Jan Hendricksen, from *Strückhausen,* in Oldenburg, acquired land in New Castle, in September 1656.

Juriaen Hendricksen, from *Osnabrück,* was at New Amsterdam as early as 1639. He seems to have been a carpenter. He is frequently mentioned in the records. In 1662 he went to Holland.

Marritje Hendricks "Van Norden" in *East Friesland,* was married January, 1656, in New Amsterdam, to Huybert Hendricksen, from Rodenkirchen.

Marten Hendricksz, from *Hamelwörden* [Hammelwarden], near Freiburg on the Elbe, Hanover, came to New Netherland on "den Harinck", July 7, 1639, and was engaged for six years as a farm hand in the colony of Rensselaerswyck.

Augustine Herrman, born in 1621 in *Prague,* Bohemia, came to New Amsterdam in 1643. He was the son of Augustine

Ephraim Herrmann and of Beatrice, a daughter of the patrician family of Redal. His father, a Protestant, was an honored citizen and merchant in the "Kohlmarkt," but was outlawed because of having been involved in certain political affairs; he then removed to Amsterdam. The son was highly educated, spoke several languages. By profession he was a surveyor. Tradition says that he took part in the Thirty Years' War before settling in New Amsterdam. He seems to have been employed as a clerk by the West India Company, frequenting the South River Country before 1643. He married in 1651, in New Amsterdam, Janneken Varleth (from Utrecht). On his own declaration he was the "first beginner" of the important traffic in tobacco between Virginia and New Amsterdam. "On his farm, near the site of the Astor Library of later years, he seems to have experimented successfully with the cultivation of indigo."

He was a member of the first "Board of Nine Men." Stuyvesant used him on many important embassies, the one of 1659, when he went to Virginia to clear the government of New Netherland from the charge of exciting the Indians against the English, becoming the occasion of his settling in Maryland.

He drew a map of the state of Maryland for Lord Baltimore, which was highly praised for its exactness, the first of its kind and printed in London in 1673. A copy of it is contained in the Grenville collection in the British Museum, adorned with Herrman's autograph and portrait. In payment for it he received a large grant of land, at the head of Chesapeake Bay, now in Cecil and New Castle Counties. This grant together with other grants he received from Lord Baltimore amounted to 30,000 acres. It was known as the Bohemian Manor. Herrman removed from Manhattan to this new manor with his family in 1661. His son Ephraim married a woman of Norwegian blood (p. 103). Both father and son were for some time interested in the project of the Labadists to found a colony. Augustine Herrman gave them a grant of land, a step which he later was sorry for. He cursed his son for becoming a Labadist.

In 1663 (1666?) Maryland by an act of legislature naturalized Augustine Herrman and his two sons — "the first act of the sort known to have been framed in any of the colonies."

Augustine kept a journal, parts of which have been preserved. Augustine's wife was a member of the Dutch Reformed church in New Amsterdam. But his name does not appear as a communicant.

Roeloff Hermansen, from *Germany*, and his wife came to New Netherland by the ship "de Vos," which sailed Aug. 31, 1662.

Barent Holst, from *Hamburg*, arrived at New Netherland in the spring of 1663 by "de Rooseboom." He was at Esopus in 1666, died 1667. A Laurents Holst figures in the court records of New Amsterdam 1668—71. Was he a brother of Barent? Could he have been a Dane? Laurents Holst and wife Hilletje Laurents were members of the Dutch Reformed church in 1686.

Adriaen Huybertsen, from *Jena*, was in New Amsterdam as early as 1660. If there were not two persons in this city by this name, he is the Adriaen Huybertsen who worked for Swartwout in Rensselaerswyck in 1637. A person by his name is mentioned in the records as fencing in farms, navigating yachts. In 1663 he was a widower, with three children. He lived in 1665 at High Street, New Amsterdam.

Reyner Van Giesen, was, judging by the name, from *Giessen*, Germany. He was in New Amsterdam in 1670.

*

Geertje Jacobs, from *Stettin*, was married, October 13, 1647, in New Amsterdam, to Geurt Coerton, from "Northhuysen in Gelderlandt." In 1657 Engeltje Mans, a Swedish woman, was fined 10 guilders for calumniating Geertje Jacobs, a woman "whom nobody would suspect." However, Geertje herself could vie with Engeltje in circulating gossip.

Herman Jacobszen, a soldier from *Emden*, married, in January, 1660, in New Amsterdam, Weyntie Martens.

Jan Jacobsen, from *East Friestland*, came to New Netherland, with wife and two children, in "de Rooseboom," which sailed March 15, 1663. He is sometimes called Intje Jacobs in the records.

Mrs. Jan Jacobsen (see above), coming, in 1663, to New Amsterdam, from *East Friesland,* in company with her husband was probably a German.

Pieter Jacobsz, from *East Friesland,* came to New Netherland by the "Bonte Koe," which sailed April 15, 1660.

Aeltje Jans, from *Bremen,* was married, in August, 1643, in New Amsterdam, to Pieter Collet, from Königsberg. Prior to this marriage she was the widow of John Cornelisen of Rotterdam.

Hilletje Jaleff, from *"Oldenburgerlandt,"* married, on July 4, 1655, in New Amsterdam, Tobias Wilbergen, from Torup in Denmark (p. 283).

Barent Jansz sailed from the Texel by "de Eentracht", Marcn 21, 1630, arriving at New Amsterdam, May 24, of the same year. He was from "Esen" ("Desens" = the man from Esens) that is *Esens,* in East Friesland. He sailed as farm servant of Brant Peelen (from Nykerck), of the colony of Rensselaerswyck. His name does not occur in the records of this colony after 1634. He was probably the first German settler in New Netherland.*

Evert Jansen, from *Emden,* married, July, 1644, in New Amsterdam, Susanna du Trieux. He acquired a lot in 1647, another

---

* Arriving by the same ship and at the same time as Barent Jansz were Pieter Hendricksz and Rutger Hendricks, both from Soest. Whether from Soest in the province of Utrecht or from Soest in Westphalia, is not stated.

There were in New Netherland before 1630 people from Germany, concerning whose nationality nothing definite can be said:

Hendrick Christiansen van Cleef (Cleves) may have been a German. He was a mariner. In 1610 or 1611 he and another mariner, Andriaen Block, chartered a ship and visited Manhattan. He later made several voyages to New Netherland, where he served for a time as factor for merchants in Holland. Late in 1614 or early in 1615 he erected the first building in New Netherland of which any valid record remains. It was, says Mrs. Van Rensselaer, a little fort or blockhouse placed upon Castle Island, which, close to the western shore, is now within the limits of the city of Albany. It was built for defense and for the storage of furs. It was protected by two large and eleven smaller cannon, and was thirty-six by twenty-six feet in size, surrounded by a stockade fifty-eight feet square and a moat eighteen feet broad. It was called Fort Nassau. Jacob Eelkins was in charge of its little garrison of ten or twelve traders during Christiansen's absences. Hendrick Christiansen was killed by an Indian.

Peter Minuit, the first General Director of a self-governed New Netherland, was also from Cleves (Wesel). Prof. Faust claims that he was a German. Mrs. Van Rensselaer says, he was of French Huguenot extraction. He arrived at New Amsterdam in 1626. It was he who bought from the Indians the Island of Manhattan for sixty Dutch guilders. Under his rule New Netherland got self-government, however, under the patroon system. This system aroused a great deal of opposition, because the patroons became manor lords, who carried on colonization as a private affair. Minuit was recalled in 1631. He left the colony in a prosperous condition in 1632. Later he became leader of the Swedish colonization at Delaware, and built Fort Christina, where he died and was buried in 1641.

lot in 1652 at Beverwyck. His name often occurs in the church registers of New Amsterdam. He died in 1655.

Evert Jansen, from *Jever,* became a small burgher in New Amsterdam, 1657. He was either a shoemaker or a ferryman.

Gerrit Jansen, from *Oldenburg,* lived at the Manhattans as early as 1635. In 1632 he had been foreman at the farm of Van Rensselaer. About 1639 he married. He had several children. He acquired ninety-two acres of land at "Pannebackers Bou" in 1646.

Harmen Janzen, from *Hesse,* married, on December 11, 1650, Maria Malaet, Angola (Mulatto?). Janzen was well versed in the Indian language. He removed to Esopus in 1661. There were two Herman Janzens in New Amsterdam. The one from Hesse probably signed the Lutheran petition of 1657, regarding Rev. Goetwater.

Hendrick Jansen, from *Jever,* acquired fifty acres of land, August 25, 1654, on Long Island, near Hellegat. A Hendrick Jansen Smith, secured a lot in New Amsterdam as early as 1644. Was he the Jansen from Jever?

Hendrick Jansen, from "Aschwaerde in't Stift *Bremen*" married, September, 1652, in New Amsterdam, Magdaleen Jans van Swol. He seems to have been a mariner, being in 1648 at Fort Nassau on the South River, 1655 at Fort Cassimir. He was a member of the Lutheran church on the South River, and requested in 1675, that two congregations, established under the Lutheran pastor Fabritius, be confirmed. A Hendrick Jansen was member of Jacob Leisler's council in 1689—90. Was he the one from Bremen?

Hilletje Jans, from *Oldenburg,* was married, October, 1652, in New Amsterdam, to Ide [?] Corneliszen Van Vorst. In 1662 she was unjustly arrested for having baked a quantity of biscuits in order to sell them. She proved, however, that she had done it for "her lying in," and was acquitted. Her husband owned land at Schreyer's Hook in 1664. He is also mentioned in the records as late as 1674.

Jan Janszen, from *Tübingen,* married June, 1649, in New Amsterdam, Baertje Hendricks Kip, from Amsterdam. A Jan Jansen signed the petition of the Lutherans in New Amsterdam, 1657. Was it the one from Tübingen?

Netter Jansen, from *Emden,* came to New Netherland by "de Trouw", which sailed February 12, 1659.

P. Jansz, from *Brunswick,* acquired fifty acres of land in October, 1653, at Catskill, and twelve more, in November of the same year. Is he and Pieter Teunizs ,from Brunswick (see art.) the same person?

Rem Jansz, a smith from *Jever* in Oldenburg, was in New Amsterdam as early as 1638, and owned land on Long Island in 1643. In May, 1650, he leased a garden near the church yard of Ft. Orange. He is the common ancestor of the Remsen family, one of whom has been president of the Johns Hopkins University.

Gertruy Jochems, from *Hamburg,* came to New Netherland by "de Trouw," which sailed February 12, 1659. She had two children along. She was the wife of Claes Claesen, from Amersfoort, who had already emigrated.

Barent Joosten, from "Wiltmont in *Embderlandt,*" married, in December, 1658, in New Amsterdam, Sytie Laurens, of Long Island. She was the daughter of Laurens Pietersen, a Norwegian. Barent had several children. In 1664 he was a magistrate.

Jacob Joosten, from *"Moesel, Graach",* in Germany, was in New Amsterdam in September, 1662 (or before), when he is mentioned as a widower.

Pieter Jordaensen, from *Lübeck,* married, July, 1642, in New Amsterdam, Catharine van Coesvelt.

Burger Joris, from *Hirschberg,* Silesia, was in New Amsterdam in 1637. For some time he worked in the colony of Rensselaerswyck. In 1639 he removed to New Amsterdam, where he, the same year, married Engeltje Mans, of Sweden (p. 329).

Burger Joris was a smith. He was one of the few inhabitants of New York who got the great burgher's right (1658). He was prominent in public life.

*

Jan van Kalcker, presumably from *Kalkar*, in Cleves, was in New Amsterdam in 1653, when he is mentioned as party in a lawsuit.

Hendrick Karstens was born in 1610, in *Oldenburg*, Westphalia. Not long thereafter his father removed to Amsterdam. Hendrick went to sea, married in 1644 Femetje Coenrats, from Gronningen. Soon after the birth of their first child they came to New Amsterdam. They took up land at Harlem. Karsten is regarded as one of the founders of Harlem. Besides being a sailor, he was a mason.

Abraham Kermer, from *Hamburg*, married, December, 1656, at New Amsterdam, Metje Davids, from Arnhem. They had several children. In 1665 they lived near the "City Wall," in New Amsterdam. In the same year they promised the government to lodge soldiers in their house. Kermer is mentioned in 1674 as sueing one Jan Raye. Metje joined the Dutch Reformed church in 1677. Abraham joined it in 1678. They lived at that time in Niew Street.

Jochem Kettelheym (Kettel), from *Kremmen*, near Stettin, Pomerania, came to New Netherland by "den Houttuyn," which sailed August 4, 1642. He worked, 1646—48, in Van Rensselaer's colony (Vlackte). He leased a farm, 1649, formerly occupied by Simon Walichs. In 1661 the records show that he resided in New Amsterdam, where he owned a house.

Hans Kierstede, from *Magdeburg*, was one of the earliest surgeons and physicians in New York. As early as 1638 he held the position of official surgeon of the West India Company. He married, June, 1642, at New Amsterdam, Sara Roelofs (p. 105), daughter of the Norwegian couple, Roelof Jansen and Annetje Jans. The present work contains an illustration showing the house of Hans Kierstede and his wife. Hans first joined the Dutch Reformed church, January 11, 1664, the church which had been served by Rev. Bogardus, the step-father of Kierstede's wife.

Jochem Kierstede, from *Magdeburg,* a brother of Hans Kierstede, secured land in New Netherland in 1647. Not long there after he perished in the wreck of the "Princess."

Styntie Klinckenborg, from *Aachen,* was first married to Roelof Swensborg, from Denmark, who died in New Amsterdam. In February, 1661, she married again, in New Amsterdam, Jan Doske, a soldier from Tongeren.

Franz Krieger, from *Borken* (in Westphalia or in Hesse), married in February, 1660, in New Amsterdam, Walburg de Silla, from Maestricht.

Barent Jansen Kunst deeded, on October 13, 1662, to Albert Coninck, half of his house and lot in New Amsterdam. The other half was owned by Claes Carstensen, a Norwegian. Kunst was a German (p. 52).

*

Jan Jansen Lammertsen, from *Bremen,* came to New Netherland by "de Bever," which sailed May 9, 1661. In 1663 and later we find him in Albany. A Jan Lammertsen [and his wife, Gretie Jans] joined the Dutch Reformed church in New Amsterdam. October 7, 1663.

Jeurian Jansen, from *East Friesland,* married June 1, 1658, in New Amsterdam. He was a cooper.

Magdalentje Lamberts "Van Tellickhuysen," of *Steinfurt,* in Münster, was married in 1661, at New Amsterdam, to Adam Dircksen "Van Colen op N. Haerlem." She was later (1663) married to the Swede (or Finn), Mons Pietersen, from Åbo.

Laurens Laurenszen, from *Bremen,* married August 25, 1669, in New Amsterdam, Hilletje Gerrits, widow of Gerrit Hendricksen.

Jacob Leisler, the best known German in New Netherland in the seventeenth century, came to New Netherland in 1660, sailing as a soldier, by the Otter (April 27). In the ship's list of passengers he is called "Jacob Leyseler, from Franckfort," probably Frankfurt am Main, to which his father, a clergyman, had been driven by persecution from the Palatinate. On April 11, 1660, he married Elsje Tymens, who had Norwegian blood in her veins, being a niece of the famous Anneke Jans, from Marstrand, Norway (pp. 113 f.) He acquired his wealth through trade with the Indians, becoming one of the richest men in New York. In 1689 he bought a piece of land, the present site of New Rochelle in Westchester County: it was a humanitarian venture in behalf of the Huguenots who had come to New York. He was a champion of civic and religious liberty. "When, in 1675, Governor Andros fined a number of burghers because of their opposition to popery, Leisler refused to pay, preferring imprisonment to the renunciation of his principles. At another time, when a poor Huguenot family landed in New York and were to be sold as redemptioners, he instantly paid down the sum demanded for their transportation, thus delivering the refugees from years of servitude." (Prof. A. B. Faust.)

When Gov. Nicholson had to flee from the country, Leisler was appointed by a committee on safety commander-in-chief of the fort and of the city, until the arrival of the new governor from England. He was finally appointed, by the same committee, supreme commander of the province. As such he made complete reports to King William, to whom he was as loyal as to the Protestant cause. On December 11, 1689, he assumed the command as lieutenant-governor. Some of the old aristrocrats were his enemies. They were captured and sentenced to death. But they sued for mercy, and Leisler pardoned them

In the course of events, they caused his ruin. Had he "employed the thorough methods of the revolutionary dictator, he would have destroyed his enemies while they were in his power, and thereby forever ended their opportunities for doing harm. This act of grace on the part of Leisler, while it elevated him as a man, was undoubtedly a political mistake." (Faust).

Meantime he was master of his enemies at home. But there were more powerful enemies abroad. The French in Canada, aided by Indians, planned to attack New York by way of the Mohawk valley and Albany. The massacre of Shenectady, often referred to in this volume, was the result. The fort was burned, the occupants were slain or taken prisoners. Albany, which formerly had refused to recognize the authority of Leisler, now recognized it. He fortified the city, and his enemies fled to the New England states.

As he perceived the value of co-operative action, he invited the governors of Massachusetts, Plymouth, East and West Jersey, Pennsylvania, Maryland, Virginia to a common congress at New York. They were to discuss plans of resisting the enemy.

The congress met on May 1, 1690. New York, Massachusetts, Plymouth, New Jersey, and Maryland took part. It was the first congress of American colonies, the first of a series that was to culminate in the Continental Congress and deliver America from England.

Owing to jealousies and misunderstandings among the leaders, the plans that were accepted, were only in part carried out. Canada was to be conquered. But the colonies failed in their attempt on land and sea. Leisler's enemies attempted to make him responsible for the failure.

He was arrested by his old enemies. They charged him with rebellion. He was convicted of high treason, and was condemned to death. His judges, conducting a sham trial, were Bayard, Nicolls, Philipse, Van Cortlandt and four Englishmen who had just arrived from England.

Leisler and his son-in-law, Milborne, an Englishman, were executed on May 16, 1691. A judicial murder was thus committed. But the English Parliament later reversed the attainder against Leisler and Milborne, and restored to his heirs his property, which had been confiscated by the crown.

In 1698 the remains of Leisler and Milborne were taken from the burial-place under the gallows to the cemetery of the Dutch Church (in the present Exchange Place). This removal was an occasion of much solemnity, 1500 persons taking part. "Prominent contemporaries in other colonies regarded the execution of Leisler as eminently unjust, Increase Mather, for instance, declaring that Leisler was 'barbarously murdered'."

Leisler, as Prof. Faust says, was conspicuous for unquestioned honesty and integrity, unflinching firmness and energy.

Of Leisler's daughters, Hester married Rynders, a Dutchman. Mary, widow of Milborne, married Abraham Gouverneur, a person of brilliant attainments. "Mary's son, Nicholas Gouverneur married Hester's daughter, Gertrude Rynders; and a son of this marriage, Isaac Gouverneur, was the grandfather of Gouverneur Morris, one of the ablest members of the convention that framed the constitution of the United States."

Mrs. Van Rensselaer's "History of the City of New York" gives about 200 pages to the treatment of Leisler.

Johannes Levelin, from *Mülhausen,* came to New Netherland by the ship "de Bonte Koe," which sailed April 15, 1660. He embarked as a soldier.

Conraet Locker, from *Nürnberg,* was among the soldiers who were to embark for New Netherland on "The Otter," which sailed April 27, 1660.

Hendrick Loef, from *Fulda* in Thuringia, married November, 1657, at New Amsterdam, Geertje Hendricks, from Zutphen. They had children. Geertje, after the death of Loef, married Caspar Luttuer, from Augsburg.

Ulrich Lupold (Leopoldt), from *Stade* in the diocese of Bremen, became Van Dinclages successor as schout-fiscal in New Amsterdam. In 1638—1639, while in the colony of Rensselaerswyck, he corresponded with the patroon Kilian van Rensselaer, who was in Amsterdam.

Caspar Luttuer, from *Augsburg,* a soldier, married in July, 1664, in New Amsterdam, Gerritje Hendricks, widow of Hendr. Loef, from Fulda, in Thuringia. She was from Zutphen.

Christian Luyersen (Carsten Luurzen), from "Ley in't Stift van *Bremen*" married, in 1665, in New Amsterdam, Anna de Vos. He joined the Dutch Reformed church April 6, 1664. He was a tanner and shoemaker.

*

Hans van Mansvelt (from Mansfeld) was in New Amsterdam as early as 1642 or before, when he had a son (Pieter) baptized.

Tryntie Martens, from *Aachen,* was married in 1658, in New Amsterdam, to Paulus Pietersen, of the diocese of Cologne.

Adolf Meyer, from *Westphalia* ("Ulfen" or "Ulsen"?), was one of the founders of Harlem in 1661. He married, in the spring of 1671, in New Amsterdam, Maritje Ver Veelen. She joined the Dutch Reformed church in December, 1673. He joined it March 1, 1674. They had ten children. Adolf had two brothers, *Andrew* and *John Meyer* who also immigrated to America.

Martin Jansen Meyer, from *Elsfleth* in Oldenburg, was a resident of Amersfort, Long Island, 1653, where he was magistrate for some years. He was a smith. In 1662 he married, in New Amsterdam, Hendrickje Hermans. They owned a house and lot in Sheep's Lane, worth about $2,150. They were Lutherans. Martin signed a Lutheran petition in 1674. They made a joint will in 1693, which was proved in 1714. Their daughter, Elsje, born in 1663, married Burger Myndertsen, smith, probably a son of Meyndert Frederickse, from Jever. Martin and Hendrickje had nine children.

Nicholas De Meyer, from *Hamburg,* was one of the most prominent among the Germans in New Amsterdam, becoming mayor of the city in 1676. The New York Genealogical Record (IX., 16) well says: "Perhaps no class among the early residents of New Amsterdam was more distinguished for the rapid strides they made to wealth and social distinction in their adopted home, than those who came from the old commercial cities of Germany. The most prominent representative of this class, which includes, among others, the heads of Van der Beeck, Santfort, Ebbing, Leisler, Schrick [They are all treated in the present Appendix] was Nicholas De Meyer."

Mr. J. Riker, in his book on Harlem [city of New York] calls Nicholas De Meyer a Dane since his native city of Hamburg was claimed by the Duchy of Holstein. In all probability De Meyer was German. In the records he is often called Nicolaes van Holstein. He and his descendants seem to have preferred the ordinary appellation of De Meyer (= steward or farmer).

He settled in New Amsterdam about 1655, marrying on June 6, 1655, Lydia van Dyck, daughter of the ex-fiscal Hendrick van

Dyke. He engaged extensively in trade. In less than twenty years he became next to Fredrick Philipse the wealthiest inhabitant of the city, his fortune being equalled only by that of one person, Cornelius Steenwyck. De Meyer was elected schepen in 1664, alderman 1669—1670, again in 1675. In 1676 he was appointed *Mayor of the city.*

He joined the Dutch Reformed church in 1660.

His wife died in 1687, leaving Nicholas five children, the eldest of whom, William de Meyer, became a prominent citizen of Esopus and Kingston in the present county of Ulster. Nicholas married again: Sara Kellenaer, a widow. He died in 1690.

Jan Meyndertsz, a farmer from *Jever*, came to New Amsterdam together with his wife by the ship "de Trouw," which sailed February 12, 1659. His wife was Belitje Plettenberg.

Marie Moores, from Aachen, came to New Amsterdam by the ship "de Trouw," which sailed December 22, 1659.

·*

Pieter Van Oblinus, from *Mannheim*, married, in 1685, in New Amsterdam, Cornelia Waldron. He joined the Dutch Reformed church in 1681. Was he of French descent?

*

Evert Pels, from *Stettin*, Pomerania, came to New Netherland in "den Houttuyn," in 1642. He was accompanied by his wife and a servant. He was a brewer, and was engaged to brew beer in the colony of Rensselaerswyck. He moved to Esopus in 1661. We find him later as a contractor for the building of sloops. His widow, Breektje Elswaerts, married again in 1678.

Albert Pietersen, "Trompeter," from *Hamburg*, married in 1641, in New Amsterdam, Marritje Pietersen (see p. 268).

Annette Pieters, from *"Brutsteen in Duytsland,"* was married August 18, 1641, in New Amsterdam, to Laurens Pietersen from Tönsberg in Norway (p. 129).

Elsje Pieters, from *Hamburg*, widow of Hans Webber, married, in August, 1650, in New Amsterdam, Matthys Capito, a German. She was killed and burnt in the Indian War of 1663.

John Pietersen, from *Lübeck,* married, in September, 1676, in New Amsterdam, Mary Brouwers, from Gauwanes.

Paulus Pietersen, from "Merven" in diocese of *Cologne,* married in 1658, in New Amsterdam, Tryntie Martens, from Aachen. They had several children.

Pieter Pietersen "van *Bremen"* acted as sponsor in New Amsterdam in 1663.

*

Oben (Abel) *Reddenhasen* [Reddinhaus], from the Principality of *Waldeck,* married December 28, 1641, in New Amsterdam, Geertie Nannincks, widow of Van Tjerck Hendricskszen. They had children. As late as 1686 his wife is mentioned in the records (Geertruy Riddenhar). He died before August 2, 1644, when his widow sold her house in New Amsterdam, at the corner of the East River and the present Broad St.

Andries Rees, from *Lippstadt,* was one of the signers of the petition of the Lutherans at Amsterdam, 1657, requesting that Rev. Goetwater be permitted to remain as Lutheran minister in the city. His wife was Ciletje Jans. Their son Johannes was baptized in New Amsterdam on April 26, 1656. Andries, on his arrival at New Amsterdam, was probably a soldier. In June, 1657, he was promoted to "the rank of a cadet." When the government desired to billet off soldiers in 1665, Andries, being approached, said he could take no soldiers, because he "is afraid of being robbed!" He was engaged in tapping in 1660 and afterwards, being several times arrested for tapping and playing at nine pins on holidays. When arrested in 1663, he admitted that he had "tapped on Sunday," but "after the preaching," what he was entitled to. Moreover, he did "no business during the week." He was liberated. In 1674 he had property on the present William St., between Hanover Square and Wall St., then known as Smith St.

Hendrick Jansen Reur, from *Münster,* Westphalia, was appointed court messenger in the colony of Rensselaerswyck in 1651. He died before February 4, 1664, when his household effects were sold at auction.

Jan Riet, from *Bonn,* was listed among the soldiers who were to sail to New Netherland by "The Otter," April 27, 1660.

Robbert Roellants, from *Berlin,* is mentioned at various times in the early records of New Amsterdam. He appeared as sponsor in 1658, arbitrator in 1661. By trade he was a carpenter. He had contracted to build a house for Pieter Kock (p. 236).

Lysbeth De Roode, from *Danzig* (wife of John Salme) and her child, three years old, came to New Netherland by the ship "de Trouw", which sailed January 20, 1664. Six months later her daughter Sara was baptized in New Amsterdam.

Daniel Ruychou (Ritsco?), from *Danzig,* married, August 26, 1661, in New Amsterdam, Catharyn van der Beeck.

*

Adam van Santen [Xanten] came to New Netherland, accompanied by his wife and two children, in "de Bruynvis," which sailed June 19, 1658.

Jacob Abraham Santvort, from Germany, came over in 1661 in "de St. Jan Baptiste." He became one of the leading men in New Amsterdam. By trade he was a tanner. His first wife was Zybe Ariaens. In 1677 he married Magdalentje van Vleet, from Bremen. In 1674 his property on High St., was valued at $5,000.

Symon Scholtz (Schultz) came to New Netherland in the ship "de Vos," which sailed August 31, 1662. He was from *Prussia.*

Paulus Schrick, from *Nürnberg,* was the leader of the Lutherans in New Amsterdam, as is seen by a letter of August 28, 1658, from the Reformed pastors in that city to the General Director and Council (see p. 88). In 1654 he was in Holland, representing the Lutherans and requesting the consistory to send

over a Lutheran pastor. He lived a part of the time at Hartford.
He and a number of other "colonists" from New Amsterdam were
the earliest settlers of Hartford, being there before the English.
The first notices of Schrick in New Amsterdam is on August 28,
1651, under which date Laurens Cornelis van der Wel gave a
promissory note to him, for fl. 361.58; again on Dec. 24, 1651,
when he appeared as a sponsor at the baptism of Warnar, a son
of Henrick Van Diepenroeck. Schrick was a merchant and free
trader, a man of wealth. On October 29, 1652, he obtained a
deed from Claes Jansen van Naerden of a lot in Pearl Street, New
Amsterdam. He acquired four acres of land at "The Kolck," in
October, 1653; again four acres at the same place, in 1662. He
is one of the few in the records of New Amsterdam who are
styled "Heer" or "Sieur." A notice of July 19, 1653, states that
he had money coming in Germany. This may have been the prime
cause of his sojourn abroad in 1654—1655, when he visited the
Lutheran consistory in Amsterdam.

Schrick married on November 29, 1658, in New Amsterdam,
Maria Varleth, widow of Johannes van Beeck. She belonged to
the aristocracy of the city. She had six brothers and sisters: 1)
Nicholas, who married Anne Stuyvesant; 2) Janneke, married to
Augustine Herrmans, a German from Prague; 3) Anna, wife of
George Hawke; 4) Catharyn, wife of Francis de Bruyn; 5)
Sarah; 6) Judith, wife of Nicholas Bayard.

Schrick had two children, Susanna and Paulus, who were
born at Hartford. But both children were baptized in New Amsterdam on the same day, September 2, 1663. Schrick died in the
same year. His widow married a third husband in 1664, William Teller.

Hans Schröder, from *Mansfeld,* married, as widower, Aug.
25, 1641, in New Amsterdam, Aeltje Jans. His first wife was
Lysbeth Jans.

Jan Hermanszen Schut, an "Adelborst," from *Lübeck,* married, December 26, 1649, in New Amsterdam, Margreta Dircx
(Denys?), a widow. They had a daughter, Fytie, baptized in 1651.
Schut seems to have traded at the Delaware river. He was killed
about 1651, when his widow married Jan Nagel. There was also
another Schut in New Amsterdam, a Williamse Schut who acted
as sponsor in 1642.

Claes Claesen Sluiter, from *Oldenburg,* was in New Netherland in 1679 (or before), when he married at Kingston.

Lucas Smith [Schmidt van Jehansberch] (van Coerlant), from *Johannisberg* in the district of Gumbinnen, in East Prussia, arrived at the Manhattans, on "den Conick David," Nov. 29, 1641. He at once entered the service of Domine Bogardus. In August, 1642, he began working in the colony of Rensselaerswyck as a farmhand and clerk. In 1646 De Hooges testified in writing that Smith was an especially pious, faithful and honest young man.

Annetje Sodelaers (Sedelaers or Sylers) from *Königsberg,* in Prussia, married, Nov. 20, 1660, in New Amsterdam, Jan Sprongh, from Bon in the province of Drenthe. Mr. Bergen's Book on Kings County, N. Y., says that she came from "Connex in Bergen, Norway." This is erroneous. Jan and Annetje had several children. The records mention an Annetie Jacobs Sprongh as being dead in October, 1670, when her widower, Matthyas de Haert, married again. Was she the wife of Sprongh, or his sister? Bergen says that Annetje Sodelaers, as widow of Sprongh, was married to Claes Teunisse Clear, in September, 1694.

Caspar Steinmetz, a German, possibly from *Berlin,* was in New Amsterdam in 1648 or before. In 1653 his wife is mentioned as having worked for Judith Verleth. Steinmetz had nine children. In 1655 he petitioned for leave to "tap beer and wine for the accommodation of the burghery and strangers," which petition was granted. In 1665 he hired his house as a city school for fl. 260 a year. However, he had trouble in collecting the rent. He removed to Bergen, N. J., where he became magistrate. In 1674 he signed a petition of the Lutherans. He died in 1702.

Johan Steffen, soldier, from *Herborn,* in Prussia, came to New Netherland on the ship "de Moesman," which sailed March 9, 1660.

Engelbert Sternhuys, a tailor, from *Soest* in Westphalia, came to New Netherland on the ship "de Moesman," which sailed April 25, 1659. He died in 1678.

Harmen Stepfer, from the Duchy of *Cleves,* came to New Netherland by the ship "de Trouw," which sailed Dec. 23, 1660. In 1662 he is called Steppe or Stegge in a deed by which Pieter Jansen (see p. 81), Norwegian, portioned off a lot for him.

Hartwick Stoeff, from *Lübeck,* arrived at New Amsterdam on the ship "Draetvat" in the spring of 1657.

Jacob Stoffelszen, from *Zürichsee,* Switzerland, came to New Netherland in the spring of 1639. In 1643 he is mentioned as purchasing a boat from Jacob Couwenhoven; in 1653 as the step-father of Annetie Cornelissen Van Vorst, whom Pieter Kock (see art. p. 233) sued for breach of marriage contract. In 1654 Jacob sued Ide [?] van Vorst, his stepdaughter, "who lays claim to half a negro." Jacob thought he should be entitled to look upon the negro as his own property. Incidentally we learn that it was a habit to give negroes as presents to the bride at weddings. Ide got two at her wedding. Jacob had a brother, Reyer, who is mentioned by the pastors of New Amsterdam as singing "German songs on shipboard" (p. 88). On August 17, 1657, Jacob married a second time: Trintje Jacobs, widow of Jacob Waelingen, from Hoorn.

Reyer Stoffelszen, a brother of Jacob Stoffelszen, was from *Zürichsee,* Switzerland. He was a smith. He was at New Amsterdam in 1638, and succeeded Burger Joris, of Silesia, as smith of Rensselaerswyck in 1639. He does not appear in this colony after 1647, but is mentioned in the records of New Amsterdam in 1653. He was dead before 1660, when his wife, Geertje Jans, was widow. A letter of the Reformed pastors in New Amsterdam, Megapolensis and Drisius, Aug. 23, 1658, says that Paul Schrick, the leader of the Lutherans in that city took Reyer to be a Lutheran "because he sang German songs on shipboard on the way to Holland." (p. 88.) This must have been about the year 1654 when Schrick visited Holland and Germany. Reyer's wife was a member of the Dutch Reformed church in 1686. She was then living at the "Deacon's House for the Poor," in Broad St.

Hendrick Sweterinck, soldier, from *Osnabrück,* was among the passengers to embark for New Netherland, by the ship "de Bonte Koe," which sailed April 25, 1660.

Herman Theuniszen, from Zell in *"Münsterland,"* married, April 19, 1654, in New Amsterdam, Grietje Cosyns. In 1659 he worked for Augustine Herrmans, from Prague, as "his farmer." Herman had several children.

Pieter Teunisz, from *Brunswick,* is first mentioned in the colony of Rensselaerswyck under date of March 28, 1648, as taking with him cattle and implements to Catskill. In 1652 and 1653 he and John Dircks of Bremen were summoned before court to settle accounts. He is also mentioned in the Albany records as late as 1684—85.

Willem Janzen Traphagen, from *Lemgo,* in Lippe, widower of Jutge Claes Groenvis, married, June, 1658, in New Amsterdam, Aeltje Dircks, from Steenwyck. By her he had a son, Johannes, who was baptized April 9, 1659. He married a third time: Joosje Willems. Rebecca who was born in this marriage was baptized at Brooklyn, Feb. 9, 1662.

*

Nicholas Velthuysen, or Langvelthuysen, from *Lübeck,* was in New Amsterdam in 1650 or earlier. He was married twice. His first wife Janneke Willems died in April, 1659, leaving children. In June, of the same year, he married Aeltje Lubberts, widow of one Bickers. Five months later they separated. He beat her, "could not live with her." He was engaged in many brawls, what his vocation, that of a tapster, invited. About 1660 Velthuysen "absconded." It was decided that his estate should be sold. In 1662 a conversation was reported as having taken place in February, 1660, on board a ship, that Velthuysen had died on a trip to "Genee."

Johannes Verveelen had property in 1674 in New Amsterdam, on the present Broad St., on South William St. and Broad St. It was valued at $3,000. In 1667 he was constable of N. Harlem, also overseer of the N. Harlem court. In 1671 he was appointed constable and clerk of Fordham. Before 1664 he and his wife Anna Tjersvelt [Jaarvelt] joined the Reformed church.

The *Verveelen* family of New Amsterdam is of German stock

with infusion of French, as Riker, the historian of Harlem, says. It came from Amsterdam.

Johan Verplanck, a smith and baker, sailed as a soldier to New Netherland by the ship "de Bonte Koe," on April 15, 1660. He was from *Bonn* "above Cologne," as the passenger list states. In 1663 Sussana Verplancken and a child one and a half year old came to New Amsterdam. Was she a relative of Johan?

Magdalentje van Vleet, from *Bremen,* was married, in 1677, in New Amsterdam, to Jacob Abraham Santvort, a German.

Hans Vos, from *Baden,* came by "den Houttuyn," August 4, 1642. He worked in the colony of Rensselaerswyck. Soon after his arrival he was appointed court messenger in the colony, a position for which he was reappointed several times . In 1658 he appeared in court in New Amsterdam, though his residence was given as Fort Orange. In 1659 he had a contract on Burger Joris' [from Silesia] bowery. He was married. In 1661 he was deputy officer at the prison in New Amsterdam. In 1675 he is again mentioned as being at Esopus.

Thomas Vorst, from *Bremen,* came to Netherland by the "Otter," which sailed April 27, 1660.

Jan Vresen, "Adelborst," from *Hamburg,* embarked for New Amsterdam in the ship the "Otter," which sailed April 27, 1660. He was accompanied by his wife and two children, respectively eleven and nine years old. A Jan De Vries, and wife [name not given] joined the Dutch Reformed church in 1677.

Jan Vreesen, from *Hamburg,* came to New Netherland in "de Statyn," which sailed Sept. 27, 1663.

*

Jan Barentsz Wemp, nicknamed Poest, was in the colony of Rensselaerswyck as early as 1643. He had charge for some time of a saw- and grist-mill, and leased land 1647—1654. Poesten Kill is named after him. He was born about 1620, probably in *Germany.* "Wemp" would suggest that he was from Vemb [Incorrect for Vem: J. P. Trap] in Denmark, but his real surname was Wimpel. A silver cup of 1657 bears the name Jan Barensen Wimpel. "The New York Genealogical and Biographical Record," XXXV., 190 f., claims that he was from Germany, adducing as proof that "Wämpel" appears as a surname in *Bavaria,* 1604. "Vimpel," can be Danish, meaning, pennant. Wemp became one of the proprietors of Schenectady. His wife was Marritie Meynderts. They had six children. Wemp died in 1663. His widow married Sweer Teunis Van Velsen. Both were slain in the massacre of Schenectady in February, 1690.

Anneke Wessels van Colen [Cologne] was married, April 19, 1654, in New Amsterdam, to Hendrick Gerritszen "Van Nes in Embderlandt." He was a tailor.

David Wessel, who signed the petition of the Lutherans, in 1657, requesting that Rev. Goetwater might be permitted to remain in New Amsterdam as a Lutheran minister, was probably a *German.* His name as well as his close association with Germans, and his creed would indicate that. He was at Midwout in 1654; acted as sponsor for a child of Andries Rees, a German, in 1656. His wife was Tietje Gomme(ls). Their daughter, Amelia, was baptized July 4, 1660. Wessel was a turner. He lived, in 1665, on the Heere Graft in New Amsterdam.

Jochem Wessel (Backer) was probably a *German.* He obtained a lot in Beverwyck in April, 1651. He was a baker. He married Gertuy Hieronimus. They had several children. In 1674 he signed a petition of the Lutherans at Willemstad requesting permission to bury their dead. As it was, they were employing their own sexton, and were obliged to pay the Sexton (Aansprecher) of the Reformed Church besides.

Vrit (?) *Wessel,* who signed a Lutheran petition in 1674, in the capacity as elder or principal of the "Augsburg Confession here" (Bergen, N. J.) was possibly a *German.*

Wessel Wesselsen, from *Münster,* came to New Netherland by the ship "de Hoop," which sailed on January 12, 1661. A person by this name is mentioned as deceased Feb. 14, 1661. A

Wessel Wesselsen is mentioned as living at Esopus in 1667, and as having a wife called Maria ten Eyck, 1672.

Jacob Barents Weyt, from *Cologne,* was a member of the Dutch Reformed church in New Amsterdam in 1649.

Hendrick Wierinck, from *Wesel,* came to New Netherland in the ship "d'Eendracht," which sailed April 17, 1664.

Geertruyd Willekens, from *Hamburg,* widow of Hendrick Gulick (Gülch, near Cologne), was married, in September, 1653, in New Amsterdam, to Claes Claesen Smitt, from Amersfoort.

Hendrick Willemse, who signed the petition of the Lutherans in New Amsterdam, 1657, requesting that Rev. Goetwater might remain in the city as Lutheran preacher, probably was a *German.* He is mentioned as early as 1648. He owned a house at the N. W. corner of the present Bridge and Broad Street. He was a baker, was appointed inspector of bakeries in 1663. He was later appointed overseer of streets. About 1670 we find him in Albany. In 1671 he and other Lutherans signed a petition complaining of their minister. His daughter, Geesje Hendricks, married Dirck Jansen van Cleef (Vanderclyf, probably from Alphen, in Brabant). Geesje had six daughters, most of them married persons of English descent.

Reinert Willemszen, from *"Oldenburgerland,"* married, April 10, 1660, in New Amsterdam, Sussanna Arents. In 1655 the property of a Christian Jacobsen Backer of Sont was at his house. Willemszen was a baker, became Schepen and Firewarden of New Orange [New York] in 1673. His property on the present south side of Stone St., between William and Broad Street was valued at $6,000.

Barnt Wittenhooft, tailor, from *Münster,* came to New Netherland by "de Trouw," which sailed March 24, 1662.

*

Andrew Christian Zabriski, came to New Netherland by "de Vos," which sailed Aug. 31, 1662. In the ship's list of passengers he is called "Albert Saborsiski, from Prussia." He was the progenitor of a prominent family of New York. Tradition says that he was a Pole. He may have been a German of Polish extraction. He had been intended for the Lutheran ministry, but as the authorities sought to force him into the army, he came to New Netherland.

Name Index

This index provides access to the first Germans in America who are referred to in the works in this volume - close to six hundred names. This index is significant for three reasons. First, it provides the most extensive list ever compiled for the pre-1683 German element in America. Second, this index should lead to further study and research of the pre-1683 German element. For example, more research needs to be done in Germany on the reasons the first Germans immigrated, especially since the homeland is, in many cases, indicated. In the U.S. more research needs to be done on these first Germans and their descendants, especially in New York and at Jamestown. Additional research should result in the discovery of additional names, also. Finally, this index is significant since it sheds light on a hitherto relatively unknown period of German-American history. Future German-American histories need to include coverage of this period. Since few of them have in the past, it is not surprising that the standard English-language American histories make no reference to the presence of Germans in America prior to 1683. German-American history, as can be seen by this work, begins not in 1683, but actually in 1608. Any German-American history devoid of these early beginnings is incomplete.

Several comments are in order on the form of the names. Many names are in their original German spelling. That some names appear Anglicized or Dutchified is not surprising, since the first Germans were settled in English and Dutch colonies, e.g. "Busch" was Anglicized as "Boush" and "Baumann" as "Bowman." The name "Gutwasser" was Dutchified as "Goetwater." Also, many of the first Germans came from northwestern Germany, where many of the names are closely related to those in Holland, but are actually Low German, rather than Dutch. Those interested in studying German-American name history further may want to consult the works of George Fenwick Jones, especially his "Identifying Germans in Colonial Documents: Germanic Philology and Onamastics as an Aid to Historians," in: Francis G. Gentry, ed., *Semper Idem Et Novus: Festschrift for Frank Banta*, (Goeppinger Arbeiten zur Germanistik, Nr. 481), (Goeppingen: Kuemmerle, 1988). Also see, George Fenwick Jones, *German American Names*, (Baltimore: Genealogical Pub. Co., 1990).